What people are saying about

ODYSSEY

"Your life is made for epic adventure. Do you trust that? I was blessed to be able to go to space a record-setting seven times, but the greatest journey I or any of us will ever undertake is the one to encounter our God of heaven here on Earth. Creative and engaging, *Odyssey* offers us a map for this kind of journey. The astronauts profiled in *Odyssey* are men I know and have known, and the book captures the very sights and sounds of their heroic stories. But *Odyssey* is also extremely practical and helpful; the exercises offered will awaken wonder and launch you into your own journey. It is a must-read for men yearning to move beyond their current circumstances and embark on the journey of a lifetime."

Jerry Ross, US Air Force Colonel (ret.), member of the US Astronaut Hall of Fame, author of *Spacewalker*

"This book is beautifully written, surprising in simplicity, utterly profound. Great stories, deep truths, and that ever-elusive *how*. I highly recommend it."

John Eldredge, president of Ransomed Heart Ministries, *New York Times* bestselling author of *Wild at Heart* and *Get Your Life Back*

"Tension and what lies on the 'other side' of it are the seeds of adventure. In the Gospels we see Jesus tell a group of men, 'Let us go to the other side.' Every man hearing his words had a decision to make: stay on the shore or head into the unknown. Those who got into the boat saw things they had never seen, felt things they had never felt, and did things they had never done. We can't speak for the others who remained on land. And that is the sad and challenging truth before us as men. We must take risks to find true meaning and to secure stories worthy of being retold. The book in your hands is going to reintroduce you to what you already know intuitively—that a safe life is a wasted life. In fact, it is the unsafe spiritual life that God is calling us into. Step away from the shore, get into the boat, and dive into *Odyssey*. It's time to start living the way you were created to live as a man."

Kenny Luck, founder of Every Man Ministries,
award-winning author of twenty-three books
for men, including *Dangerous Good* and *Risk*

"Riding helps me live in the moment. It's a way to find myself, worship, and ask God the big questions. *Out there*—surviving the adventure, discovering where the road goes—we wrestle through things. God brings me into alignment with truth. Gently, he encourages me to get right with my fellow man. To be open to failure. To fix the things that aren't lined up in my life. To get unstuck. And to dream about what's beyond. Riding brings me into oneness with someone of infinite wisdom, someone who loves me with infinite love. *Odyssey* will help you find your own adventure. And *out there*, you'll find him too."

Tom Ritchey, adventurer and legendary builder
of bike frames, inventor of the first production
mountain bike, founder of Project Rwanda

"We have lost our sense of wonder. We have become cynics and skeptics. We work to achieve, yet hope eludes us. Loneliness is everywhere, and love slips through our hands. Justin Camp's *Odyssey* will restore awe and wonder in your life. His book will help you find a God who is mysterious, wonderful, personable, and inviting. Using real-life stories from one of man's greatest feats, space travel,

Justin invites you into the yet-to-be-discovered adventures that are available to all of us with our awesome God."

Troy Mangum, creator of *The Kindling Fire* podcast, inspiring listeners to live in calling, mission, and message, author of *Fatherhood Faceplants*

"There is a longing in the heart of every man. Deep, core, unquenchable by human effort. *Odyssey*, by Justin Camp, leads us into what that longing is, why it is there, and how to meet it. Saddle up for an epic adventure of the heart! You won't return the same. I didn't."

Chris Hartenstein, director of The New Frontier, a ministry guiding fathers and sons into deeper relationships through service, solitude, and adventure

ODYSSEY

ODYSSEY

ENCOUNTER THE GOD OF HEAVEN
AND ESCAPE THE SURLY BONDS
OF THIS WORLD

JUSTIN
CAMP

ODYSSEY
Published by David C Cook
4050 Lee Vance Drive
Colorado Springs, CO 80918 U.S.A.

Integrity Music Limited, a Division of David C Cook
Brighton, East Sussex BN1 2RE, England

Library of Congress Control Number 2019948097
ISBN 978-0-8307-7876-8
eISBN 978-0-8307-7915-4

The Team: Wendi Lord, Michael Covington, Stephanie Bennett, Paul Pastor, Megan Stengel, Kayla Fenstermaker, Jon Middel, Susan Murdock
Cover Design and Illustration: Nick Lee
Cover illustration based on image from Getty Images

Printed in the United States of America
First Edition 2020

1 2 3 4 5 6 7 8 9 10

030220

To Jenn, John, Bryan, Julie, Terel,
and all the others who helped
make that one journey possible.

Deep calls to deep.

— a longing of man

This is eternal life, that they know you, the only true God.

— a prayer of Jesus

CONTENTS

BEFORE YOU START

Man is made to journey. It's in our bones to feel the call, a yearning to go. For it's *out there* that we get to experience the unpredictable, the inspiring, the indescribable. *Out there*, we mature and change. *Out there*, we become our fullest selves.

Out there, we find home.

But in our present culture, more and more of us are getting stuck. Sometimes it's fear. Often it's confusion—especially because of all those promises our modern culture makes about finding esteem and security and comfort from created things: a job, a title, an accomplishment, a balance in a bank or brokerage account. So, instead of spreading sails wide and striking out for new horizons, we spend decades staring at the same old walls. And when those promises come up empty—and they always come up empty—we don't know where to turn.

Well, I'm going to tell you where to turn.

My friend, it's time to start thinking bigger.

■ ■ ■

As you read this book, you'll encounter half a dozen nano-histories—short profiles of six astronauts. Six fascinating mortal men. Six fearless and frail spacemen who undertook unthinkable journeys to unimaginable places but lived lives not unlike yours and mine—lives mixed up between the yearning and the going and the stuck.

Each astronaut here hails from NASA's legendary Mercury, Gemini, and Apollo programs—from the midcentury golden days of the space age. These men went higher, farther, and faster than any human before or since. And their journeys to outer space provide fine opportunities to learn about the greatest journey any of us can ever undertake—the most thrilling of all adventures, the most fulfilling of all expeditions: to go *out there* and discover the God of heaven somehow; to begin to develop a personal relationship with him; and to come home changed, ready to begin life on Earth anew.

It's to this great journey that we must now turn. We must, that is, if we're finally ready to live bigger lives. *Lives ignited.* Lives burning with energy and purpose, joy and peace, kinship and community. Lives beyond self-centeredness and self-doubt. Lives beyond bogged or beaten or benumbed. Lives "to the full" (John 10:10).[1]

Sometimes great journeys are literal; sometimes they're figurative. They always have a spiritual component but oftentimes physical components too. Noah jumped into a boat. Abraham hit the road. Moses marched into a desert. David and Peter and Paul—they each shared in multiple crazy cool adventures with God.

Hear and trust me. God's inviting *you* into this kind of journey right now—even in the midst of your busy modern life. What is it? What will it look like? Well, that's what this book is all about. What you hold in your hands is a practical field guide. It offers a path to follow. It comes fully equipped to equip you for the road ahead—helping you overcome objections and discover the journey that God's handcrafted just for you.

So gather round, and let your God-given adventurous heart be roused by stories of daring and heroism. And be inspired to undertake an odyssey of your own. If you do—if you go—you too will have stories to tell. And your life will *never* be the same.

I promise.

Justin Camp
San Francisco Peninsula

The first astronaut nano-history comes in chapter 2; my story starts things off. And each chapter opens with a short piece of creative nonfiction. Because some details from the lives of these midcentury space travelers have been lost, I reimagined certain scenes, reconstructing them in ways that reflect the essence of actual events and qualities of their character. As you read these pieces, hunt for the themes represented therein. Those themes are what the corresponding chapters are all about. And at the end of each chapter is a section entitled "On Board." With simple exercises, these sections turn the focus to you. Take your time with them. It's these sections that will guide you along ancient paths toward freedom and goodness … and God.

HIGH FLIGHT

Oh! I have slipped the surly bonds of Earth
And danced the skies on laughter-silvered wings;
Sunward I've climbed, and joined the tumbling mirth
Of sun-split clouds—and done a hundred things
You have not dreamed of—wheeled and soared and swung
High in the sunlit silence. Hov'ring there,
I've chased the shouting wind along, and flung
My eager craft through footless halls of air …

Up, up the long, delirious, burning blue
I've topped the wind-swept heights with easy grace
Where never lark nor ever eagle flew—
And, while with silent lifting mind I've trod
The high untrespassed sanctity of space,
Put out my hand, and touched the face of God.

// John Gillespie Magee Jr., World War II pilot

C

001

CARBON AND BLUE SKY AND HOME

A man fits shiny steel into a slot with a sharp click. He fumbles and finds the loose end of the belt and pulls, tightening it around his waist. He relaxes against the armrests and pushes his feet forward, stretching and pressing his sore body into the seat back. He settles into the void—into the *nothing* he needs to do for the next two hours.

He squeezes his hands into fists and opens them; he scans a cut, a scrape over there, and a small puncture from a thorn on his thumb. But his mind is somewhere else.

Before long, twin GE engines crank and begin throwing fourteen thousand pounds of thrust. He turns his head to the brightness of the window. Runway slips past.

As the plane lifts into the air, the man straightens. His eyes survey the seats in front of him—the bulkhead, the overhead bins, the seat belt signs. But his conscious mind registers none of it.

He closes his eyes and feels the increased g-force in his chest. Way more dramatic, though, is the increased gratitude in his heart.

I'm a son.

A close friend sits beside; another across the aisle. But he holds on to his words. It isn't a moment for conversation. He just rests in fullness. The fullness of a trip home. The kind one experiences returning from a sacred journey—from a place not marked on any map.

Opening his eyes after a few moments, he looks again out the window. He watches rural Montana blur as it gets farther and farther away.

The world seems different somehow. Bigger. More wonder and opportunity. But safer too.

Is this how things were supposed to be all along?

With his gaze still on the land below, the man's attention drifts inward, backward. His mind settles on a few specific moments, a few precious moments, only hours ago on the north face of a low mountain. A volcanic peak among several rising together—the tallest reaching about three thousand feet. A cluster of small islands floating in a great prairie sea.

He summons the smells, the sounds, his view from where he'd taken cover in front of a scrubby tree. He sees the view north across the border into Canada, west across the land of the ancient Blackfoot to the ragged, mystical peaks of Glacier National Park.

The airplane bumps and climbs, but he enjoys a moment of stillness—soaking in love and recalling his experience, hunting for mule deer, in the presence of God.

He and his friends covered a lot of miles on this trip, carbon bows in hand. But there were long hours of silence too—and prayer. And this man isn't much used to that. His friend, though, the one seated next to him, had challenged him to embrace the solitude—to make use of it.

He stifles a chuckle as he thinks about their conversation a couple of weeks back about the solitude this kind of adventure offers. It'd started with the recollection of words from an old hunter long gone: "The best camouflage pattern is called 'Sit down and be quiet.'"

His friend had surprised him then by saying that he takes advantage of his sit-down-and-be-quiet time by praying, hour after hour. It sounded daunting. But it piqued something too. Because God had been awakening something in the man's heart of late, he recognized it for what it was: an invitation. Into what, he didn't know. But he accepted it and spent the better part of a week hiking, running, crouching, crawling, and talking to his Father God.

They'd hunted in the mornings, starting out before dawn, and in the afternoons, staying out until after dark. And through it all, he did his best to remember to pray—and listen.

Those prayers—mixed with some adventure, the wonder of God's creation, and a respite from the demands of home—worked to put the man in a position that was mostly unfamiliar. It was a position—a spiritual posture—that allowed him to receive *more.* It put him into position to have a fresh encounter with God himself and with God's outrageous love.

And it was undeniable. Over the course of those days and over the trails in those mountains, he'd heard whispers. Whispers from a good, strong Father to a beloved son. He'd felt God's love in the rocks and slopes and trees and skies. In the sound of frost under his boots. In the kiss of afternoon breeze on his face. In the hand signals and knowing looks exchanged by friends in the field and the laughter and meaningful conversations back at the lodge each evening.

And then the man *really* felt his Father's love on that final morning—when it all happened. When he experienced the oddest, most unexpected thing. When he, from beside that scrubby tree, encountered that improbable and magnificent white-tailed buck.

The man knew—before, during, and afterward. He just knew that he knew. After having spent four days close by his Father's side, he just knew it in his heart.

That place and those moments were gifts just for him.

Once the memories and sensations have run their course, the man closes his eyes. Deep within, underneath the sound of the raging turbofans, he does something he's never done before: he considers what he knows for sure, the things he can hold fast to in this crazy world. He counts and considers them. Things he's experienced. Things he's been told by people he trusts. Some things he's read. He turns these truths over and over and around.

There aren't many. And most involve God. Because he follows God and always has, in some way or another. He can't remember a season when he didn't go to church. Even in high school and college and his postcollege years, when the culture of the world directed his steps. Even then, he'd somehow find his way to church. Most of the time, at least, if not always *on* time.

So he's heard lots of sermons—and until now, he thought he knew all the most important things there were to know about God.

But this right now. This is something different. This is new.

And I don't want to lose this.

Exhilaration eclipses peace as it becomes clear that he's going to have to contend with a brand-new truth—one that's very likely to become the most important of all.

The aircraft continues its ascent, pushing toward the ragged clouds above the grasslands becoming foothills becoming mountains—and this brand-new truth descends, pushing down, down from his head, down toward his heart.

Chasing that beautiful deer, back there and below, was amazing. It was one of several dozen great experiences he's had in his forty-plus years. *We weren't even looking for whitetail!* But that isn't it. The truth headed for home is this: this man's God in heaven loves him. *Him.* Not all humans, with him thrown in, as he's always thought. But *him.* And he always has. *A lot.* Way more, in fact, than the man could have ever imagined.

As he sits there in seat 8D, exhilaration gives way to true joy as his heart grasps the fact that God had been dreaming about this very day for eons, that he handcrafted the details of it in breathless anticipation, that he delivered each instant with precision and delight. And that he did it all with the pure and singular purpose of giving his boy a sense—just a sense—of how much he's loved. This small, undeserving son of God.

The man sits still, comfortable in the uncomfortable seat, and revels in outrageous love.

I never want to lose this.

The jet bounces and lurches and breaks through the thin layer of clouds into bright sky above. Sun glints off the fuselage; contrails stream from the tail. And this new truth sinks deep into the dark reaches of the man's heart, brightening things there.

He's starting to see God as his very own Papa.

He's beginning to see himself as Papa's beloved son.

And he knows somehow that this is the beginning of something big.

■ ■ ■

That was me. Awestruck, heart aflame, but at peace too. And at home—though still a thousand miles from my physical home in Northern California.

Have you been there? Does this story resonate? Do you know God with this kind of longing and satisfaction?

I confess, until recently I couldn't relate. And I know most churchgoing men in our modern world won't connect with these words either. We'll nod our heads about God's love *generally* or *theoretically*. But we don't know much about the scale of God's love for each of us *specifically, personally.*

Something isn't connecting.

Maybe you're the exception. Maybe you've grown to know God as "good, good Father," as the great song goes.[1] Maybe you've grown to know him as someone who loves you so much, he can't turn his adoring gaze away, no matter what you've done. As someone whose fierce love will never change, no matter what mistakes you've made, no matter what sins you've committed.

But most of us today don't know him like that.

Because that would require a journey we've not yet made.

■ ■ ■

God is Elohim—Creator of heaven and the earth. He is El Shaddai, El Elyon, and El Olam—God Almighty, Most High God, and Everlasting God. He is the Alpha and the Omega—the first and the last, the beginning and the end. These ancient names of power, drawn from the original languages of the Bible, are as true today as they have ever been.

But, just as much, he is Immanuel—God with us (all the time); and he is Abba—Dad, Papa (all the time). And we *must* get to know him in these intimate ways too. We must.

I will show you how.

■ ■ ■

Sunday mornings in my leafy hometown in Silicon Valley usually meant my family was at church. My mother, a Midwesterner, was tall and thin with ash-blond hair. A former teacher, she had a sharp mind and a soft heart. But most of all, my mom loved God. It was she who encouraged our church attendance—and gently enforced it.

Our church was medium sized, Presbyterian, and perched on a hill. I wouldn't say it was thriving, but it had a certain momentum—young families, a fine pastor, picnics, vacation Bible schools, pancake breakfasts, and Christmas Eve services lit by flickering candles.

Our Sunday routine was simple. My parents would drop us at our classrooms, walk down the hill to the sanctuary, then return an hour or so later.

I was two years old when we arrived in California from Colorado and began this pattern. My sister was five. As we got older, my sister and I and other kids would start in the sanctuary, stay for part of the service, then head upstairs for the remainder of the hour. But in middle school, my parents offered us a choice: we could continue going to Sunday school or stay in the sanctuary for the entire service. We never went to Sunday school again, but we missed few sermons. Mom saw to that.

Later, when I moved to Los Angeles for college, I continued going to church—sometimes with friends, mostly by myself. Then I met a girl. Her name is Jennifer. (We still go to church together, if you know what I mean.)

After we graduated, we got married. And we attended church together most Sundays too—first in Center City, Philadelphia, then in Morningside Heights, Manhattan, then in Menlo Park, California.

During those years, sermons were my connection to God. They were my window into who he is—and who I was. And those sermons offered a ton of truth. I learned to look to the Bible as my authoritative guide, inspired by God himself. I learned that God exists as Father, Son, and Holy Spirit. I learned that Jesus died sinless and rose again—offering himself as a sacrifice, saving us from sin and death.

These are good truths. They went in deep, and for them I am supremely grateful. But not everything I learned was so great. Somehow those decades of well-meaning preaching also taught me—sometimes explicitly, sometimes implicitly, but always in ways I understood—that God often didn't approve of me or really understand what I was going through. Those sermons gave me the nagging feeling deep down that he was disappointed—sometimes even disgusted—with what I was. With who I was.

They implied in no uncertain terms that he wanted me to do better at following the rules. (*I will; I promise.*) They taught me that I needed to be a better person. (*This time I'm going to be.*) They taught me that I just needed to man up. (*I will try my best.*)

And with it all, something else became clear—that I wasn't going to be able to deliver on any of my promises, not perfectly. Instead, a deep realization came, so quietly I couldn't sense it was a lie.

I've got to get better at hiding the less-than-perfect parts of me. If I don't, I'll never belong. Not to God. Not in this world. Not in my own skin.

And I wanted to belong. I wanted to be home.

■ ■ ■

I never doubted I was a beloved son—my mom's. When I got into trouble in middle school and high school (and I did plenty), she stood with me. Her love never wavered. But it wasn't like that with God. His love and acceptance always seemed to vary according to how I acted or failed to act. So, growing up and far into adulthood, rather than a beloved son of God, I felt more like an orphan.

Just so you know, God has taught me since that his is the only unconditional love there is—and that it was his love, actually, that was flowing through my mom. But I sure didn't understand that at the time. Because while I'd heard a thousand stories of him, I can't remember many from that season that revealed what his heart is *really* like.

So, for much of my life, I had a warped view of God—and myself. I didn't know of his attraction and attentiveness toward me, uniquely, in every moment.

I didn't know. And the omission stunted my maturity in every way. I became a striving man hiding nearly constant and medium-level sadness and anger and cynicism.

Because here's the thing: without an inkling of how much God loves us, even in our darkest moments, the good news of the gospel isn't so good, is it? I mean, if God is disapproving and disappointed, sometimes disgusted, that's actually bad news, right? It sure seemed that way to me.

Yes, I thought, *Jesus died for me. Yes, I'm going to heaven. But do I really want to? Do I want to spend all that time with someone like* that*? To go to a place run by a guy who doesn't even like me—who maybe even considers me repugnant?*

And *repugnant* was an easy jump. Because when I was twelve, a doctor told my mother she had leukemia. And with that pronouncement (and the "everything's now out of control" feeling that came with it), I grabbed the stick. I grabbed the yoke.

I began trying to control everything in my life. And I did it in the ways my young mind could come up with: by dulling pain and fear with food and friendships and by breaking rules and questioning authority. And when I got a bit older, it was with achievement in school and my careers—but with food still and then pornography too.

God wasn't the only one who sometimes thought I was repugnant.

So here's what I told him: "I believe in you. But I'm going to *live* for something else. The world, quite frankly, offers news that's better than yours. I hear culture telling me if I work hard, if I don't screw up too badly, then I can find all the security and comfort, peace and happiness I'll ever need. Praise and respect too. If I'm lucky—maybe lots."

And I told God, mostly with my actions, "If you won't stand with me when I struggle, if you won't have my back when I mess up—as any good father should—then I'll father myself. I'll protect and take care of myself." And I did. I tried, at least. And then in my twenties, I told him, "I'll protect and take care of my family too."

It's up to me. My strategies. My solutions. Because I'm alone.

But then, around my forty-third birthday, my Father in heaven apparently decided it was time to do something about my beliefs (which, by that time, had become worn) and with my vows (which, by then, had become overworked).

And what he did—honestly but figuratively—left a big, smoking hole in the ground.

■ ■ ■

A few months prior to that trip to Montana, I'd asked a question that had seemed fairly ordinary. In prayer one Tuesday evening, I asked God whether there were any lies I was believing about him or about myself. And in the silence that followed, my mind settled on a specific conclusion I had reached in the weeks and months after my mom's long-ago diagnosis. In prayer I pictured myself back then, alone in my bedroom just after my parents had relayed the doctor's news, my young mind landing here: *God must love me less.*

As an adult in my forties, I'd learned enough to know—on an intellectual level, at least—that my youthful conclusion was inaccurate. But it still somehow stuck, and it still *felt* true, even years later, as I sat in that chair with my eyes shut, my imagination surrendered in prayer.

So, in that moment, having had enough of those old feelings, I decided to renounce my long-ago conclusion. I told God, simply, I didn't want to believe it anymore—not about him, not about me.

And I said "Amen." And promptly forgot about it all.

But God didn't.

Looking back, I can see it now. That prayer was the first step in a grand expedition—a pilgrimage into God's heart. It marked the start of a great journey, one that included a hunting trip but would become so much more. It was the beginning of the kind of odyssey we all must undertake if we want to experience true intimacy with God.

An Odyssey—like the one in that old Greek tale about a legendary adventurer. His was a journey for the ages—gods and monsters. But you know what?

All he really wanted was to find his way home.

TITANIUM AND BRIGHT STARS AND WONDER

The capsule is tiny. Almost *too* tiny.

Now, the rocket that carried the capsule up here and on which it sat until moments ago—that's what you'd expect. A giant ballistic missile named Atlas—the titan from Greek mythology. A behemoth with a belly full of rocket fuel and liquid oxygen, spitting 360,000 pounds of fire and fury straight down.

But that giant's gone now—falling, spent, doing slow cartwheels back over there somewhere. And this thing here? This thing is a tin can. A titanium, beryllium, chromium, molybdenum can, actually. But a can nonetheless. A tiny metal can.

It's barely big enough for a man to fit in. And if a guy's taller than five feet eleven, he ain't going to. The capsule is so small, in fact, that the few men who've been inside have been known to crack wise that "you don't get in it, you put it on."[1]

And a man did put it on today. And he and the capsule are all alone now, hurtling through space at more than seventeen thousand miles per hour. Outside the walls of the can is death—by speed, by cold, by void, by radiation.

The man inside is too well trained, though, to be focusing on the horrors that would rush in if those walls somehow failed. No, he's in the groove, busy working. Marking checklists, reading instruments, pressing buttons, turning dials, and communicating with his team back on the ground. But in the few and brief moments between those duties—and there are a few—he takes time to delight in the wonder of this strange place and this singular moment that Atlas bore him up here to experience.

For this man's heart hungers for wonder. And right now, as he and the capsule pass from night into day—his heart thrills to the brilliance of the first of three sunrises he'll see today from the vantage of Earth orbit. But he's about to see something else. Something beyond what he or anyone else expected for this flight. Something he'll never quite be able to explain.

[Transcript of MA-6 Air-Ground Flight Communications]

Astronaut: *"This is Friendship Seven.... The sun is coming up behind me in the periscope, a brilliant, brilliant red. Over."*

Mission Control: *"Roger."*

Astronaut: *"It's blinding through the scope on clear.... I'm going to the dark filter to watch it come on up."*

Mission Control: *"Roger."*

[And here it comes, the surprise ...]

Astronaut: *"I'll try to describe what I'm in here. I am in a big mass of some very small particles that are brilliantly lit up like they're luminescent. I never saw anything like it. They round a little; they're coming by the capsule, and they look like little stars. A whole shower of them coming by.*

They swirl around the capsule and go in front of the window, and they're all brilliantly lighted. They probably average maybe 7 or 8 feet apart, but I can see them all down below me, also."

Mission Control: *"Roger, Friendship Seven. Can you hear any impact with the capsule? Over."*

Astronaut: *"Negative, negative. They're very slow; they're not going away from me more than maybe 3 or 4 miles per hour. They're going at the same speed I am approximately. They're only very slightly under my speed. Over.*

"They do, they do have a different motion, though, from me because they swirl around the capsule and then depart back the way I am looking.

"Are you receiving? Over.

"There are literally thousands of them.

"This is Friendship Seven. Am I in contact with anyone? Over."[2]

The man in the capsule, grasping for words, is John Glenn.

■ ■ ■

The mood of the country was tense in those days. After the second of two horrible wars finally ended, a new threat had emerged. Just after World War II wound down, the Cold War began, and our Soviet allies turned quickly into our prime adversaries. Their hostility, sometimes brazen, sometimes sly, caused deep national anxiety about the spread of communism and the prospect of all-out nuclear war.

Four years, four months, and sixteen days before Glenn's 1962 flight, the Soviet Union launched *Sputnik*—Earth's first artificial satellite. It was about the size of a disco ball, orbited Earth every 96.2 minutes, and went *beep-beep-beep.*

Lyndon Johnson, then Senate majority leader, always unvarnished, expressed the concern of our nation: "Soon, they will be dropping bombs on us from space like kids dropping rocks onto cars from freeway overpasses."[3]

President Dwight Eisenhower responded by establishing NASA—the National Aeronautics and Space Administration: "To provide for research into problems of flight within and outside the earth's atmosphere."[4]

Eisenhower wanted to beat the Russians. He didn't want just to get a *thing* into space; he wanted to get one of *us* there. So one of NASA's first programs was commissioned to do just that. Project Mercury's goal was to launch a man into Earth orbit and recover him safely.

John Glenn would be that man. He was made for it, after all.

Glenn was born in the hills of eastern Ohio, as all-American as they come. "As a boy," the editors of *Time* magazine wrote, "Glenn swam in Crooked Creek, hunted rabbits, played football and basketball, read Buck Rogers, was a great admirer of the big-band musician Glenn Miller and blew a blaring trumpet in the town band."[5] At a small local college, Glenn studied chemistry, played football, and flew small airplanes in a civilian pilot training program.

When Japan dropped bombs on Pearl Harbor, though, he left college and went to fly for the Marine Corps. He would complete fifty-nine combat missions in the Pacific theater of World War II—another ninety in the Korean War. After that, he became a test pilot. He took his piloting skills to Patuxent River, Maryland, and began pushing the envelope of what man and machine could do in the wild blue. He tested navy and marine jet fighters—planes with names like FJ-3 Fury, F7U Cutlass, and F8U Crusader.

And when the United States needed to make up ground in the space race, Glenn was a clear choice to help. Out of 508 qualified candidates, he was among seven men chosen by NASA for the Mercury program. And he stood out even among that vaunted group: "He had the hottest record as a pilot," wrote Tom Wolfe.[6]

Glenn was accomplished and confident, both in himself and in his preparation. He had faith in science and engineering. He trusted them so much, in fact, he was willing to face the prospect of death at supersonic speed. But he had faith in something else too—something beyond physics, bigger than human ambition, larger even than the possibility of atomic annihilation.

John Glenn had faith in God.

The faith of his Scotch-Irish family and forebearers had grown strong in him. A few months after his famous Mercury-Atlas 6 flight, evangelical magazine *Christianity Today* called his faith "rugged and unshakable."[7]

For decades after, though, he was forced to live out that faith not in space but on the ground. Mercury-Atlas 6 had rejuvenated American confidence and made Glenn a hero. President John F. Kennedy awarded him the NASA Distinguished Service Medal—and promptly grounded him. He'd become "so valuable to the nation," said NASA administrator Charles Bolden, Kennedy wouldn't "risk putting him … in space again."[8]

So Glenn used his Earth-bound hero status to speak about his flight—and about his faith. But Glenn didn't stay grounded permanently. At age 77, in 1998, near the end of a long career as a US senator from Ohio, he joined the STS-95 mission crew on space shuttle *Discovery*. And once more, the world got to see his heart for wonder. During a news conference from orbit, Glenn radioed back, "To look out at this kind of creation out here and not believe in God is, to me, impossible."[9]

■ ■ ■

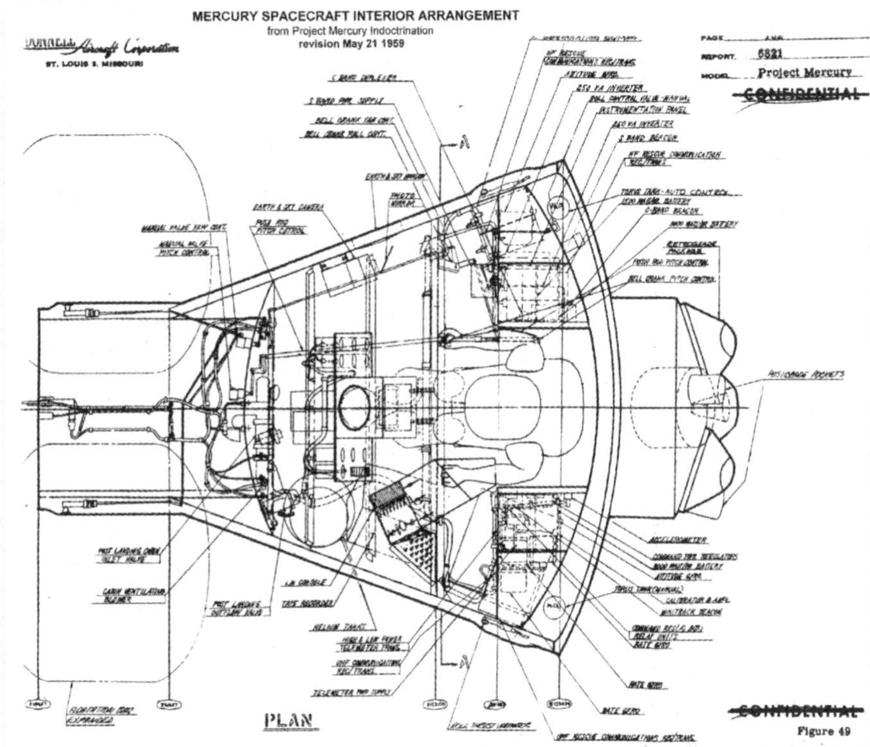

A Schematic of the Mercury Capsule

QUESTiON:

"IS THERE MORE GOING ON HERE?"

You may have asked ... Isn't heaven a place we go when we die? Isn't being a Christian just about doing good; going to church; reading the Bible a bit; and, most of all, believing in Jesus—so we make darn sure heaven ***is*** *where we go?*

You may have asked ... This life's about what we can see, hear, and touch, isn't it?

These are great questions, and the truth will blow your mind. **Think bigger.**

■ ■ ■

As the scientific revolution (1500s and 1600s) rolled into the industrial revolution (1700s and 1800s), then into the information age (1900s and 2000s), crazy breakthroughs in science and technology turned our collective gaze toward the natural world and away from the supernatural realm.

Little by little, discovery by discovery.

Men like Isaac Newton, Charles Darwin, Albert Einstein, Enrico Fermi, Francis Crick, and James Watson pioneered breathtaking theories that enabled us to understand and explain the mechanics of our physical world—and of the larger cosmos. These revelations, along with some cascading social currents, resulted in a new cultural mind-set—one in which God and heaven and worship and prayer gradually began to seem somehow less immediate, less relevant, less essential. The idea that there might be something beyond the observable, something more basic than space and time and matter, began to strike many people as improbable. The idea that there might exist a spiritual reality beyond, above, beneath, and intermingled with our physical world became sort of quaint.

Speaking at the Seattle World's Fair just months after Glenn's Mercury flight, Episcopal priest and Manhattan Project physicist William Pollard, a man *Time* magazine dubbed the Atomic Deacon, explained the shift this way: "It is an inevitable property of the people who live in any golden age to be so passionately devoted to the spirit of their age that all other aspects of reality extraneous to it are excluded."[10]

That exclusion is what most of us have done, each in our own way. The naturalists and humanists among us went ahead and rejected everything spiritual. They refuse to recognize the supernatural. They've just decided that none of it is reality at all. They've decided that, given our abilities to discover, God and heaven and the rest have become "unnecessary."[11] They've asked, "What role is there for God?"[12]

A philosophical naturalist considers us physical beings and nothing more. He or she believes the natural world, the physical cosmos, is all there is. A philosophical humanist believes that humans are capable, in and of themselves, of discovering truth and devising ways—using the scientific method and reason—to meet all human needs, to answer all human questions, and to solve all human problems. They, like naturalists, reject the idea that there is anything beyond the physical world.

The atheistic beliefs underlying naturalism and humanism originated in the ancient world but began to have wide cultural influence in the seventeenth and eighteenth centuries. Then they morphed and matured and increased their impact in the nineteenth century. And in our time, in the twentieth and twenty-first centuries, these beliefs have come to dominate many of the cultures of our world.

What's *real*, our world has decided, is whatever we can see and hear and touch—and anything transcendent to our physical reality is simply less real (or not real at all). We've raised this belief to the level of pseudolaw or pseudoreligion. It's become an "everyone knows that" kind of thing.

We Christians are neither naturalists nor humanists, at least not in the philosophical sense. But we live in (and work in and raise our families in) a culture that's influenced heavily by naturalistic and humanistic ideas and ideals. And it's easy for us to get distracted and forget and begin acting like functional atheists.

Most of us have, indeed, just like naturalists and humanists, adopted an intense bias toward the physical world. We may *believe* in a spiritual realm. We may *believe* in God and heaven and worship and prayer. But we believe *more* in the here and now.

Much more.

■ ■ ■

"Our trouble is that we have established bad thought habits."[13] And things have just gotten more unbalanced since 1948, when the great gospeler A. W. Tozer wrote those words. We go to church on Sundays—maybe—but we put virtually all our energy and time and worry toward the physical world. Work. Money. Pastimes and entertainments. The spiritual realm gets what's left, if there is anything.

Because the here and now is greedy and relentless. Demands and deadlines at work. Requests and responsibilities at home. Pressures to keep up and get ahead. These things are in our faces. We see them—email inboxes overflowing, to-do list items calling for attention. We hear them—mobile phones ringing, meetings at work never ending. And we feel them—texts and reminders and notifications buzzing, stress building.

"The world of sense intrudes upon our attention day and night for the whole of our lifetime," continued Tozer. "It is clamorous, insistent and self-demonstrating … assaulting our five senses, demanding to be accepted as real and final."[14]

Compared with this barrage, and with the busyness and hustle we muster to meet the barrage and survive as best we can, the spiritual realm can seem as if it's a million miles away. It can become, in our minds, simply something we'll (hopefully) experience someday. When we die. When we finally leave this physical, in-your-face world behind. *But not now.*

■ ■ ■

In my teenage years, God offered me a few hints that there might be something beyond this workaday world. He did so through my mom. She told me stories of a deeper, unseen reality. She spoke of praying with men and women with serious mental disorders like schizophrenia. She talked about a trip to Argentina, where she saw schools and companies and prisons transformed by truth and love and prayer. She told me about hearing gentle whispers of God in moments of stillness and silence. And, of course, she told me about praying for healing from her leukemia.

(I prayed for that too, desperately.)

When she spoke about this stuff, she talked with quiet passion. She'd seen things, been part of things—things that were beyond any here-and-now explanation. She'd experienced mystery and beauty and glory. And it changed her. It was obvious.

But, by the time she died, during my freshman year in college, I'd pretty much forgotten about all that. By then, I too had developed one of those intense biases toward the physical world—toward classes and grades, grad school and future career opportunities. By that time, for me too, the spiritual realm seemed but a distant twinkle.

■ ■ ■

"It's a rare day I don't think about it, relive it in my mind," Glenn said many years after his three orbits around Earth.[15]

He loved being in space. He loved discovery. He loved using science and engineering to go faster and farther and higher, to discover ever more about the physical world. But he also loved discovering things deeper and unseen.

John Glenn Uses a Photometer to View the Sun during Sunset on the Mercury-Atlas 6 Spaceflight

Glenn's heart was open to the whole of reality, not just part of it. He didn't let cynicism or street smarts or book smarts close off his heart. He didn't let the cultures of combat in the Marine Corps or of flight test at Naval Air Station Patuxent River or of the halls of the US Congress harden his heart.

Even when he looked at the physical world, he often tried to peer *through* it. He wanted to see the brilliance of the supernatural, even in small things:

> All my life I have remembered particularly beautiful sunrises or sunsets.... I've mentally collected them, as an art collector remembers visits to a gallery full of Picassos, Michelangelos, or Rembrandts.

> Wonderful as man-made art may be, it cannot compare in my mind to sunsets and sunrises, God's masterpieces.[16]

His most treasured of these, no doubt, were the sunrises he saw from outer space.

And then there were those crazy "fireflies." Glenn saw them on all three swings around the planet in 1962. He said the experience was "like walking backwards through a pasture where someone had waved a wand and made all the fireflies stop right where they were and glow steadily."[17]

He didn't see them on his 1998 shuttle flight, though. And other astronauts became convinced they were frost crystals that had accumulated on the exterior of his capsule.[18] A NASA astronomer surmised they were dust particles, and a physics professor said it was probably dust or loose paint.[19] And they probably were—one of those things, at least.

But Glenn was never so sure. Joining a few of his Mercury brethren for a panel discussion at the National Museum of Naval Aviation in 2002—forty years after his original flight—he talked again about those fireflies. He said, for him, "their glowing luminescence remains a mystery."[20]

As C. S. Lewis wrote, "You cannot go on 'explaining away' for ever: you will find that you have explained explanation itself away. You cannot go on 'seeing through' things for ever. The whole point of seeing through something is to see something through it."[21]

Glenn surveyed and studied our physical world. And through it, he glimpsed the mystical.

■ ■ ■

In a village named Bethany, not far from Jerusalem, Jesus had three good friends—two sisters, Mary and Martha, and their brother, Lazarus. It's possible Jesus had known the family for a long time and might have stayed with them when visiting Jerusalem for religious feasts.

One time, when Jesus was across the Jordan, the sisters sent a runner with an urgent message. Lazarus was in grave physical danger. "Master, the one you love so very much is sick" (John 11:3).[22]

Jesus did love Lazarus—and Mary and Martha too. But he didn't leave for Bethany right away. He "stayed on where he was for two more days" (v. 6).

I think Jesus delayed because he saw things from a larger perspective. Mary's and Martha's focus, understandably, was on the natural world—on the potential physical death of their beloved brother. Jesus, though, saw and sensed the whole of reality. He could appreciate his friend's physical peril, of course. But he also knew that everything on Earth happens within an even larger reality, one more elemental even than space, time, matter … and death.

And Jesus wanted to give Mary and Martha and his followers sight of it. He used their circumstances to show them (and us)—in an unforgettable manner—the presence, the goodness, and the glorious power of this deeper, unseen reality.

"It will become an occasion to show God's glory," he said (v. 4).

When Jesus finally did reach Bethany, he found Mary and Martha grieving. They wept because Lazarus, by that time, had died.

Jesus wept with them and asked, "Where did you put him?" (v. 34).

"Master, come and see" (v. 34). "It was a simple cave in the hillside with a slab of stone laid against it" (v. 38).

Jesus then surprised them: "Remove the stone" (v. 39).

"Master, by this time there's a stench," warned Martha, focusing again on the physical reality. "He's been dead four days!" (v. 39).

"Go ahead, take away the stone" (v. 41).

They did. And Jesus prayed to his Father. Then he shouted, "Lazarus, come out!" (v. 43).

And Lazarus did come out, "wrapped from head to toe" in graveclothes—but alive (v. 44).

■ ■ ■

The Bible we claim to believe in—and to base our lives on—describes, quite clearly, a deeper, unseen reality. It describes a reality that somehow preexisted the space-time continuum. It describes a deeper, unseen reality that never began, actually, and will never end. "The things that are seen are transient, but the things that are unseen are eternal" (2 Cor. 4:18).

The Bible describes a deeper, unseen reality to which time and space and matter owe their very existence. It's this that our everyday physical reality is dependent on. Time and space and matter were "called into existence by God's word, what we see created by what we don't see" (Heb. 11:3).[23]

This deeper, unseen reality is more vast, more wild and wonderful than the physical world. It is distinguished by majesty and mystery, goodness and love—"glory beyond all comparison" (2 Cor. 4:17). It's a reality where anything can happen. Even the impossible. In it, even death itself can be undone.

And it's not just out there somewhere, out in the beyond. It is there, but it's here too. Right here. Right now. "The coming of the kingdom of God is not something that can be observed," explained Jesus, but it is already in our midst (Luke 17:20–21).[24] This deeper, unseen reality is interwoven with everything in the physical world. It "holds everything together" (Heb. 1:3).[25]

And we can discover it. This reality. We can explore it. Experience it. Take part in it.

■ ■ ■

"There are other dimensions involved than just time and space," wrote Wernher von Braun, the man who developed the Redstone rockets that launched the first two manned Mercury missions.[26] "Our life does not have materialistic and intellectual aspects alone," he declared.[27]

While we may have grown more comfortable with (and confident in) the physical world, that doesn't mean we don't have spiritual aspects too. We do. For "God is spirit" (John 4:24). And he made us "in his own image" (Gen. 1:27).

God formed Adam, the first man, from the natural world—from "dust from the ground" (Gen. 2:7). But he breathed himself into Adam—he "breathed into his nostrils the breath of life, and the man became a living creature" (v. 7). He created us as physical beings. But he created us as spiritual beings too—*just like him.*

And our spiritual nature is our essence. It's what distinguishes us from the rest of creation: that we can access and experience and participate in this great reality that lies beyond our everyday reality. We're made for it; we're made to be sustained by it.

We're made to be sustained by the natural world, of course—by air and water and food and all the rest. But we are made to be sustained by the supernatural world too. Jesus taught us about "living water" and "the bread of life" (John 4:10; 6:35)—deeper kinds of sustenance that come from his deeper, unseen reality.

"Anyone who drinks the water I give will never thirst—not ever. The water I give will be an artesian spring within, gushing fountains of endless life" (John 4:14).[28]

"Anyone who eats this Bread will live—and forever!" (John 6:51).[29]

But we don't believe it. Not really.

Modern men and women, argued Pollard, have "lost all effective contact with the supernatural."[30] Long unused, our abilities to access the spiritual realm have atrophied. We've tried to opt out of the whole of reality. But we're made for life "to the full" (John 10:10).[31] And "full" requires that we experience *all of it.*

Just as our physical bodies wouldn't survive or thrive without air or water or food from the physical world, our hearts can't thrive without spiritual, supernatural sustenance either. We need mystery and wonder and beauty and glory and love overflowing.

Without them, our hearts break. And so do our lives. No wonder we're anxious, depressed, addicted, and overmedicated. No wonder we're full of doubt and cynicism, materialism and desperation.

Open the news; look at the state of the world. *Look at the state of us.*

When we believe there's nothing bigger, better going on here, we lose heart. We become mercenary, trying to pull more and more from the physical world—money, status, connectedness, whatever.

But that doesn't work either, not well enough. Nowhere near well enough.

■ ■ ■

"There's far more here than meets the eye," confirmed the apostle Paul (2 Cor. 4:18).[32] Like the luminescence of those mysterious particles, the brilliance of this deeper, unseen reality is shining all around us—every day, in every moment, just waiting to be discovered. And it "will come alive to us," wrote Tozer, "the moment we begin to reckon upon its reality."[33]

We don't have to wait until we die. God is inviting us to come and see it for ourselves. He's inviting us to come and discover and explore. *Now.*

He's inviting us to come and encounter *him*.

Because that's what all this is *really* about. Glenn once wrote, "Although we can't weigh and measure God in scientific terms, we can feel and know Him."[34] Accessing, experiencing, participating in the supernatural realm is really about encountering and experiencing and knowing nothing less than God himself.

So that's what we're going to jump into in the next chapter—knowing the God of heaven *personally*.

Do you want to? Are you curious? Then, keep reading.

■ ■ ■

— ON BOARD —

"OTHERWORLDLY"

002

You're built to experience life physically *and* spiritually. To experience the fuller life God means for you, you must begin embracing both realms. You must begin experiencing and partaking in *all* of reality—no longer just part.

You are, therefore, invited into a season of encounter. Of practical experience in the spiritual realm. If you'll accept it—or are even just curious—then jump on the questions below. They'll be your first step toward *more*.

Consider these questions and jot down your responses.

002.1 How skeptical are you, right now, about the spiritual realm and your ability to come into contact with it? Pull out a pen or pencil and circle a number below:

<< Pretty doubtful - - - - - - - - - - - - - - - - - - Not doubtful at all >>

1 2 3 4 5 6 7 8 9 10

If you *are* skeptical, what's the source of that doubt? Can you identify a particular experience or influence? Write a few sentences, if you can, that trace the source.

Also, consider this: Would you be willing to put skepticism aside while reading the rest of this book? Just to see what might happen if you do?

002.2 Spend a few moments considering your life so far. What spiritual experiences come to mind? Have you experienced anything you can't quite explain? Something you suspect was an answer to prayer or an encounter with God. Have you ever glimpsed or sensed this deeper, unseen reality?

Use that pen or pencil (or your phone) to write down whatever comes to mind. Don't filter. And if nothing comes, that's perfectly okay. Just keep moving. Keep reading.

002.3 Think about an average day. What percentage of your energy and time and worry is devoted to physical endeavors and particulars (i.e., nonspiritual things)?

<< Very little - Very much >>

10% 20% 30% 40% 50% 60% 70% 80% 90% 100%

002.4 What pressures and demands characterize your life right now? What, specifically, keeps you busy? What commands your attention?

Make a complete bulleted list.

002.5 How do you feel about this invitation to experience more of the spiritual world, more of the supernatural realm? Are you feeling eager, excited, optimistic? Are you feeling relieved, reassured? Or anxious, confused, overwhelmed, unsettled, unsure, skeptical? Are you feeling challenged, intimidated, inadequate, offended?

Describe your feelings. Capture them on paper—and you have full permission to be honest.

Pray right now:

> *God, help me see your brilliance. Teach me to slow down. Help me put skepticism and cynicism aside. Teach me to notice and appreciate. Give me a new perspective on my life and my environment. Change my heart. Help me see and hear and feel with my heart, even in the midst of the busyness and clutter of my physical world. Come into my heart and make space. Space for wonder. Space for beauty. Space for stillness. Space for life.*
>
> *Amen.*

Experiment with listening prayer.* Find a place where you can sit still comfortably for twenty to thirty minutes. The quieter the better. Somewhere outside would be good, but any place will do. Invite the Holy Spirit to direct your thoughts. Pray against distraction, against fatigue, against confusion. Now, remain quiet for a length of time—whatever feels right. Just breathe and relax. Enjoy the moments of solitude. Then, when you're ready, take a full five minutes to look at your surroundings. Consider whatever is in front of you right now. *Whatever* it is. What do you see? What do you notice? Take it in. Describe it in one or two sentences. Jot them in a journal or in a note on your phone.

When you're done observing, do it again. Take another five to ten minutes to look again. To look harder. Consider what's underneath whatever you see. What's going on beneath? Above? Beyond? What's the deeper truth? Don't rush it. And again, in one or two sentences, describe what comes to mind.

---

* For a full explanation and discussion of listening prayer, please refer to chapter 3 in the first book in the WiRE Series for Men, *Invention: Break Free from the Culture Hell-Bent on Holding You Back.*

Now, do it one more time. Spend another five to ten minutes looking again. Looking even harder. Deeper. Further. It'll be uncomfortable. You might feel like *I've done this already*. But push through. Stay with it, and ask, *What is God trying to show me here? What's he trying to give me now? What's he trying to teach me today? How is he trying to guide me? To love me?* And whenever you're done, again, in a few sentences, describe what came to mind.

Now, take a few more minutes to sit quietly. Then, whenever you're completely done, test what you've written against Scripture—invite a mature believer to comment, if you think it would be helpful. Ask, does what I've written, especially during the second and third rounds of observation, align with biblical principles? Do these deeper truths align with God's teaching in the Bible? If so, tuck them into your heart. Return to them over the course of the next few days. Consider them. Then reconsider them.

Make sure to keep good notes. As you work through these "On Board" sections, make sure to collect and preserve your answers, thoughts, and the things you think you might have heard from God. This is precious data.

ALUMINUM AND BLACK SMOKE AND LOVE

"We're finally doin' it!" the boy says, delighted.

He's twelve—and the parachute harness is way too big.

A voice crackles in his headset. "You ready, son?"

"Yes, sir." You bet he's ready. He'd be flying airplanes off carriers right now if he were only a few years older. It's 1942, and the war in the Pacific is raging.

"Okay. Here we go. *Contact!*"

grrrrunk … grrrunk … grunk … grunagrunagrunagruna …

Six hundred horses begin racing. It's loud, and the boy loves it. Black smoke blasts from the exhaust stacks. It makes him feel grown up—even though about all he can see is the interior of the cockpit and a massive engine beyond, now rumbling at the sky.

They taxi out to the far end of the runway, and the man turns the airplane. The boy revels in this invitation—this initiation—into his dad's world.

"All right, Edward. Here we go." From the rear cockpit, he eases the throttle forward—and the AT-6 begins to roll.

The airplane picks up more and more speed. A nice, satisfying growl (*mmmmmmrrrrrowwwwrrrr* …) becomes a wonderful, terrifying howl (*mmmMMMMMRRRRROWWWRRRRR* ...) as the Pratt & Whitney engine really starts to crank and the Hamilton propeller goes supersonic.

The boy has watched planes take off and land his whole life—but this is nuts. The roar permeates his body. And it's not just the noise. It's the jolting too. And it's not being able to see out of the plane's greenhouse-style canopy. All of a sudden, he feels a lot more like a kid than the full-grown man his pilot's seat is designed for.

It all feels totally out of control.

But it isn't. Because his dad is here. And he is a lieutenant colonel in the US Army Air Forces—he's got a full set of controls in the copilot's seat, and he can fly *anything*.

When the plane reaches eighty-five miles per hour, enough lift builds under the wings, and the plane begins to want to rise. It bounces on its wheels. *Like a basketball*, the boy thinks.

And then they're up. The boy's first flight.

The AT-6 Texan is a trainer. A two-seat, single-engine, low-wing monoplane built with lots of aluminum to save weight and increase performance. Sturdy and rugged, it's known as the Pilot Maker. It's a workhorse that's launched the careers of many great fighter pilots.

And it's doing its thing again *right now*.

Father and son and craft climb to 4,500 feet and level out. And the ride gets smooth. And the boy can see out! He can see everything—the sky, the clouds, the ground, way out ahead.

The man eases the throttle back.

Then, after a moment, in his headset ... "Son, take the controls."

"Really?"

"Yup. Go ahead. Like we talked about."

The boy settles his feet on the left and right pedals. He reaches for the stick and puts his left hand on the throttle. He puts a bit of pressure on the pedals and the stick, not enough yet to change the direction of the airplane—just enough to feel his control.

"Go ahead. Ease into a turn. Just how I told you."

The boy moves the stick and presses a pedal, and the aircraft banks to the right. As it does, the boy slides the throttle forward a bit.

"That's good … good. Okay, now straighten 'er out. Good job maintaining altitude."

The boy's nerves are gone. And he doesn't feel so small in the cockpit anymore either. He feels comfortable. His father gives him pointers, but he makes each movement, each adjustment himself. And his actions are small and smooth.

Pilots say when you get used to the AT-6, the plane can read your mind. And the boy seems almost used to it already as these two climb and turn and dip over the Central Lowland of southwestern Ohio.

The man in the back is delighted to be this boy's father. He would write these words many years later, cherishing the memory of this first flight with his beloved son: "He seemed to know, instinctively, that a good pilot doesn't strap himself into a plane; he straps the plane onto himself. He really flew it."[1]

■ ■ ■

By 1963, after six successful manned Mercury spaceflights—*Shepard//Grissom//Glenn//Carpenter//Schirra//Cooper*—the United States turned its attention to Project Gemini. NASA sandwiched Gemini between Mercury and Apollo, and its aim was to build on prior accomplishments and pave the way forward by developing and demonstrating certain capabilities necessary to embark on NASA's most audacious goal: the mission of Apollo—to land a man on the moon and return him safely to Earth.

The capabilities needing mastering were these: astronauts needed to be able to spend longer periods in space (long enough for the trip to the moon and back); they needed to be able to dock two orbiting spacecrafts; and they would eventually need to be able to exit one of them (to conduct experiments and collect samples on the moon).

NASA hit its stride during Gemini. It averaged one manned mission every four months during Mercury. During Gemini, things accelerated to one every two. And as a result, it was during that period the US overtook the Soviets in the space race.

Gemini is a Latin word meaning "twins." The folks at NASA chose the name because the new project would use two-man spacecraft and two-astronaut crews. To handle the larger, heavier Gemini capsules, NASA also employed a new launch vehicle. The Titan II rocket was fifteen feet taller than Atlas, and it delivered seventy thousand pounds more thrust.

NASA also needed a fresh crop of astronauts to accomplish its ambitious new goals. So, in the fall of 1962, the agency announced the New Nine.

Among these young men was a pilot named Ed White—the boy who flew that AT-6 with his dad two decades prior.

White's father, Edward H. White Sr., was a career military man. He would retire as a major general. Young Ed grew up, therefore, moving from base to base. And he learned about hard work and self-discipline, honor and patriotism—but fun and laughter too. His dad was that kind of dad.

For college, White went to West Point and afterward enlisted in the US Air Force. He spent three and a half years at Bitburg Air Base in Germany, flying fighter jets—the F-86 Sabre and the F-100 Super Sabre. And it was while he was in Europe that he read about NASA's astronaut program; it was there that he decided he wanted to go for it.

Lacking the requisite engineering degree and experience as a test pilot, he got busy. He returned stateside, earned a graduate degree from Michigan, and enrolled in the test pilot school at Edwards Air Force Base—the epicenter of the flight test world.

So, by the time NASA went looking for nine new astronauts, White had all the right stuff. "When he became an astronaut in 1962," *Life* magazine wrote, the "old hands from Project Mercury picked him as 'the guy to watch.'"[2]

White's specialty would become "the design and development of spacecraft flight control systems."[3] He described it as involving "the pilot's own touch—the human connection with the spacecraft and the way he maneuvers it."[4] It was exactly what he'd proved he had a knack for, years before, during that first flight with his father.

White's first NASA flight was Gemini IV, the first American multiday spaceflight. On June 3, 1965, he and James McDivitt blasted off from Cape Kennedy in Florida.

Beaming with love and pride, White's father chatted with reporters on the ground about his son and about the young man's prowess as a pilot. "A lot better one than I was," confirmed the retired two-star general—a man who himself was "rated to fly everything from bombers to balloons."[5]

Then, on their third orbit, one hundred miles up over Hawaii, White and McDivitt did something really kind of unimaginable. They grasped the handle of the capsule's hatch and pulled. And popped it open. Because this flight would also mark the first time an American would attempt to leave the confines (and safety) of an orbiting spacecraft.

With space suit on, White stood up and peeked out. Then he went ahead and slipped out of the capsule, out into space—tethered only by a twenty-five-foot golden cord, which supplied oxygen and a communications link.

White: *"Okay. I'm out."*
McDivitt: *"Okay. He's out. He's floating free."*[6]

Though traveling some 17,500 miles per hour at this point, White felt neither the sensation of speed nor the sensation of falling. He felt no wind—because there's no air. What he did feel, though, was the exhilaration of being the first American to walk in space.

Ed White Performs the First American Space Walk on June 3, 1965

And, it turns out, he felt something else too. His friend the Reverend Jackson Downey of First Methodist Church in Cocoa Beach, Florida, recounted that White also sensed "the presence of God."[7]

White: *"This is the greatest experience I've … it's just tremendous! Right now I'm standing on my head, and I'm looking right down, and it looks like we're coming up on the coast of California."*[8]

White's sojourn was scheduled to last twelve minutes. After more than fifteen minutes, amid all the excitement, McDivitt remembered to check back in with flight control:

McDivitt: *"Gus, this is Jim. Got any message for us?"*
Mission Control: *"Gemini IV, get back in!"*
McDivitt: *"Okay.... They want you to come back in now."*
White: *"Okay. This is the saddest moment of my life."*[9]

After twenty-one minutes, White was finally back inside the spacecraft.

The two men would complete sixty-six orbits and cover 1,609,710 miles before reentering Earth's atmosphere and splashing down in the Atlantic Ocean.

"I'm proud of my boy," said Edward White Sr. "You could tell by his voice that he was having the time of his life out there—rolling and tossing and having a great time."[10]

■ ■ ■

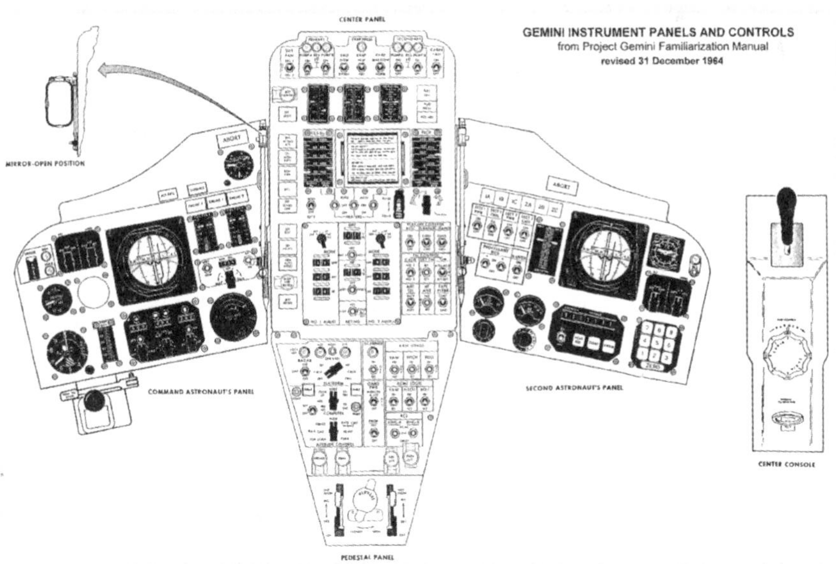

Gemini Instrument Panels and Controls

QUESTiON:

"IS RELATIONSHIP EVEN POSSIBLE?"

You may have asked ... How could it be that God wants a personal relationship with me? With billions of other humans here on planet Earth? And how would it work? Isn't he busy elsewhere, working on things more consequential?

You may have asked ... Does God even know (or care) I'm here?

These are great questions, and the truth will blow your mind. **Think bigger.**

■ ■ ■

We are living in a golden age of science, technology, and discovery. In the last hundred years, we split the atom and mapped the human genome. We invented TVs, PCs, GPS, Wi-Fi, and AI; microwave ovens and mobile phones; rockets and robots. We detected gravitational waves and inferred the existence of dark matter. We sent twenty-four men to the moon—and spacecraft to the far reaches of our solar system. We even sent two NASA probes—*Voyager 1* and *Voyager 2*—beyond the confines of our solar system; they are, right now, speeding through interstellar space.

We've gotten good at this stuff, and we're only getting better. And it's made us a bit arrogant.

Our "universe is a machine governed by principles or laws," declared Stephen Hawking, acclaimed cosmologist of Cambridge—and those laws "can be understood by the human mind."[11] Somewhere back there, way before this golden age even got going, we humans started believing that, by exploring and observing and experimenting and by engaging our brains and thinking rationally, there's nothing we can't grasp, nothing we can't accomplish, given enough time.

But there's a problem. None of this *figure-it-out-ability* works if what we're trying to grasp is God. You see, while he *is* present in this physical world—he *is* in the here and now—he also exists outside it, beyond it, above and below it.

"I am the Alpha and the Omega," says our Father God, "who is and who was and who is to come, the Almighty" (Rev. 1:8). His greatness, his riches, his understanding, and his judgments are "unsearchable"; his ways are "inscrutable" (Ps. 145:3; Isa. 40:28; Rom. 11:33; Eph. 3:8). His love "surpasses knowledge" (Eph. 3:19). The "skies—the entire cosmos!—can't begin to contain him" (2 Chron. 2:6).[12]

God will *never* fit into Hawking's machine.

How could he? How could the Creator of our mind-bogglingly massive and ever-expanding universe be so small? He is infinite, eternal. He had no beginning; he will have no end.

And so, for us, God will always be a mystery. A wonderful, gigantic, *sacred* mystery.

And *that* kind of mystery is different from a run-of-the-mill mystery. A sacred mystery, taught Richard Rohr, that cheery contrarian Franciscan, is not that which is "unknowable" but rather that which is "inexhaustible."[13] He meant that the more we discover of God, the more there *will be* to discover—*forever*.

"As the heavens are higher than the earth, so are my ways higher than your ways and my thoughts than your thoughts" (Isa. 55:9).

But some of us have a hard time with those facts. In our drive to gain understanding (and certainty and control), we as a species have lost some of our willingness to accept and appreciate mystery. Mystery offends our pride a bit because it runs counter to our faith in ourselves.

So, instead of accepting and appreciating (and reveling in) the sacred mysteries of God, many of us choose a different approach: we try to reduce God to something we can cram into Hawking's machine.

The naturalists and humanists among us, those who demand to be able to understand a thing—empirically, intellectually, fully—before they'll consider it real, simply dismiss him (or try to). They cannot comprehend God's presence in our physical world, so they try to reduce him to nothing.

We Christians don't take things quite that far. We believe there's a spiritual realm. But we too hold a strong bias toward the physical world. Because we cannot see or hear or touch him with our physical senses, we struggle to grasp that God really is here, in every situation, in every moment, in our very beings; that he really is supremely interested in each of us; and that he really is outrageously loving.

And because of that struggle, many of us try to reduce God by relegating him to the spiritual realm. We try to reduce him by turning him into a theoretical god. A million-miles-away god. An only-in-heaven god. (I've done that.)

Philosophers and theologians use a watchmaker or clockmaker analogy to explain this idea. God, the thinking goes, long ago spoke this astonishing and intricate universe into being, put it into motion (wound it up like a vintage watch), and promptly set it down. Leaving the cosmos to operate on its own, according to laws, not love.

This watchmaker idea of God, in all its nuanced versions, is common. It's why so many men in the church today believe God to be unknowable, indifferent, engrossed in more important things. We accept that he exists, that he is somehow essential to our lives (or to life in general), but we just don't believe that a personal relationship with him is possible—certainly not one that's *deep*, *real*, *heartfelt*, and *conversational*.

The data shows it. Eighty percent of Americans say they believe in God or a higher power.[14] But only 15 percent of American men say they believe that their God is both loving and interested in their daily lives.[15]

So we do what anyone would do who believed such things. It's impossible to have an authentic relationship with a theoretical god, so we turn our faith into *vitamin* faith. We shrink faith to a set of practices we should definitely try to remember to engage in—because they're good for us. We narrow our faith lives to a set of things we should for sure put on our to-do lists: ☑ go to church … ☑ attend a men's group … ☑ get some quiet time in the mornings.

Scripture says, "Listen for GOD's voice in everything you do, everywhere you go" (Prov. 3:6).[16] But we don't. We don't look for him in our everyday lives—we see only physical people and physical things. We don't listen for him—we hear only the roar of culture. We don't try to sense his Spirit within us, and we have a hard time seeing him in others—we connect instead with our drivenness and self-contempt, our envy and cynicism and judgment.

N. T. Wright, with insight and punch, wrote this: "It is our blindness, our arrogant refusal to admit of any reality that won't go into a test-tube, that prevents us from opening ourselves to God's dimensions of reality."[17] It's our refusal to accept and appreciate and revel in sacred mystery that prevents us from building personal relationships with him.

But the God who said, "Come to me" (Matt. 11:28) and "Seek my face" (Ps. 27:8), is still saying that—but to us now. He's saying that to *you*.

And the God who said, "Ask, and it will be given to you; seek, and you will find; knock, and it will be opened to you" (Matt. 7:7), meant it as encouragement to *you*.

And the God who said, "I stand at the door and knock. If anyone hears my voice and opens the door, I will come in to him and eat with him, and he with me" (Rev. 3:20)—he's making that offer to *you* right now.

God is the same as he's always been. He hasn't changed because we made some great strides in understanding our world. He holds the very "same position in our modern world that He held before we began probing His creation with telescope and cyclotron," wrote von Braun.[18]

God has always wanted us to explore and appreciate and unravel. "It is the glory of God to conceal things, but the glory of kings is to search things out" (Prov. 25:2).

But what God wants *most*?

What he wants most is personal relationships with us. *With you.*

■ ■ ■

After Ed White's triumphant space walk, NASA assigned him to the very first of the Apollo missions—along with Virgil "Gus" Grissom and Roger Chaffee. But tragically, one month before their February 21, 1967, scheduled launch, during a practice run through countdown procedures, faulty wiring ignited a fire. Before the astronauts could escape, an inferno engulfed the pure-oxygen-filled Apollo 1 capsule.

All three men were killed.

White's father was devastated. In the weeks following the accident, his tender heart moved him to compose a letter to his grandson—to White's fourteen-year-old boy, Eddie.

> Dear Eddie: This is one of those evenings when I've been thinking a lot about you. These past weeks have been hard for all of us; it takes a lot of love and courage to get through a time like this. I know you and your mother and your sister have plenty of both. But I think it helps if all of us keep in close touch, exchanging thoughts and feelings and memories. I know it helps me.
>
> Earlier, your grandmother and I were looking at a scrapbook of clippings about your father's career....
>
> As I leafed through that scrapbook, your father's characteristics seemed to jump at me from every page.

The older man went on to detail, with pride, what he knew about the son he loved so much. He wrote about his confidence. He wrote about their time in that AT-6 trainer so many years before. He wrote about his determination, his integrity, his sense of duty, his love for his country, and his optimism. And he wrote about his son's faith in God.

Guideposts magazine published the letter. Olin Teague, member of the US House of Representatives and chairman of the Manned Space Flight Subcommittee, called it "a masterpiece."[19] Teague was so affected, in fact, he put it into the *Congressional Record*. He wanted this raw and rare snapshot of a father's love to inspire others.

■ ■ ■

The kind of relationship God invites us into is the father-son kind. God made us his sons. His *actual* sons.

"Long, long ago he decided to adopt us into his family" (Eph. 1:5).[20] "Just look at it—we're called children of God! That's who we really are" (1 John 3:1).

You are his beloved son. I am too. We have all the rights, privileges, and authority of true sons. And he loves each of us "in the same way" that he loves his begotten Son, Jesus (John 17:23).

The very reason God made us, actually, was to have someone—lots of someones—to love. He made us in his likeness. He wired us like him—down in the deepest, the basal places of us, down in our machine language, down in our DNA.

"You and I are in little (our sins excepted) what God is in large," wrote A. W. Tozer.[21] And because we're like him, "we have within us the capacity to know Him."[22] God made us a kind after his kind so we would be able to come together with our kind and with him—to *be* together, to *love* one another.

That's what's real. *That's* your Father's heart. You are chosen. You belong. God is your Father. You're his beloved son. And he wants a relationship with you—deep, real, heartfelt, conversational.

■ ■ ■

Nearly eight billion people live right now on planet Earth. And God's deepest emotions toward each of us are the same. Each of us is vitally important. He loves all of us outrageously. He knows the number of hairs on each of our heads (Matt. 10:30).

Jesus used a first-century example to give us a sense of his Father's heart:

> What man of you, having a hundred sheep, if he has lost one of them, does not leave the ninety-nine in the open country, and go after the one that is lost, until he finds it? And when he has found it, he lays it on his shoulders, rejoicing. And when he comes home, he calls together his friends and his neighbors, saying to them, "Rejoice with me, for I have found my sheep that was lost." (Luke 15:4–7)

One sheep among ninety-nine is, statistically, "not very interesting," remarked Henri Nouwen, a man who wrote much and well about God's love. One person among 7.7 billion is much, much less so. "But for God," Nouwen noted, "numbers never seem to matter."[23] What matters to God is humans. Individual humans. Individual hearts. *Yours and mine.*

Like the shepherd in Jesus' parable—and like Ed White's father—there's nothing God wants more than to be with you. To love you. And there's no loving thing he won't do to make that happen—to bring us into relationship with him.

■ ■ ■

A few months after that Montana hunting trip, I was with some friends at a retreat at a ranch in the mountains of Colorado. One of them, Joel, is a musician. During some downtime, we were talking and hanging out, and he pulled out his guitar. He sat on a couch and sang a song he'd written and would soon release.

The song is called "Sons and Daughters." It's written in the voice of God—and five lines in, it goes like this:

> I sing and dance when I'm thinking of you
> And I'm always thinking of you.[24]

In that moment, Joel's voice and lyrics and God's grace pierced my doubter's heart.

Sitting there, looking out across the Colorado River, north toward the peaks of the Arapaho and Routt National Forests, I began to believe it … *for me*. In that moment I just knew that I knew. Not just intellectually. Not theoretically. And I accepted those words—and the sentiment behind them—into even the somber and shadowy places of my heart.

God's love isn't some theoretical, million-miles-away kind of love. It's up in our business. It's raw and fierce and tender and full of joy. "His desire for you and me can best be described as a *furious longing*," wrote that warmhearted, clear-sighted Franciscan Brennan Manning.[25]

God's love burns bright and hot and true. It will never dim. Not ever. Not even a little. If you were to plot his love on a graph, the line would be high and flat. It wouldn't fluctuate over time; it would never swing in response to our actions, even our worst.

You couldn't plot his love, of course. No one could draw a y-axis that high or an x-axis that long. No page, no screen could ever come close to depicting his love. It's massive and relentless.

In the seventh century BC, the prophet Zephaniah told the people of Jerusalem about God's nature—about his love for those who seek him. Zephaniah wrote that God "will rejoice over [us] with gladness," that "he will exult over [us] with loud singing" (3:17). And the word *exult* is a translation of a Hebrew word that means "to spin round (under the influence of any violent emotion)."[26] My friend Joel was right. God is so crazy in love that he sings over us. Dances because of us.

He's consumed; he can't take his eyes off us (Ps. 34:15). He thinks about us all the time. Not for a second has he ever forgotten even one of us (Isa. 49:16). There are so many thoughts about each of us in his head they can't be counted (Ps. 40:5). His love for you, for me, is so great that it's literally immeasurable and unfathomable by our human minds (Eph. 3:17–19).

Did you know that?

Do you *feel* that?

■ ■ ■

In aerospace engineering there's a concept called the "flight envelope." A flight envelope defines the limits of an aircraft's (or spacecraft's) performance capabilities—speed, altitude, and maneuverability. Test pilots, like John Glenn at Patuxent River or Ed White at Wright-Patterson, force their crafts to their breaking points—or, hopefully, just shy. They probe the outer limits of engineering and physics. They call it "pushing the outside of the envelope."

A key aspect of any airplane's flight envelope is its altitude ceiling. That is the maximum altitude at which it can maintain level flight. It's the altitude at which the engines are just barely able to generate enough thrust (and lift under the wings) to keep the plane level in the thin air. At that altitude, pilot and craft can climb no farther, for the engines are, by definition, maxed out and have nothing more to give.

■ ■ ■

Everyone needs a dad. Just as White needed his dad that day in the AT-6. Sons need to be around their dads. They need to know them. They need to be initiated into their dads' worlds—to work and play there. They need to walk next to them—to talk with and rely on them. Sons need to live in the provision and under the protection of their dads' love.

Sadly, it doesn't always work like that—but it's how things are *meant* to work.

And it's the same with God.

We often think what we need is a rescue, a way out, our prayers answered, our circumstances changed—but what we *really* need is something infinitely bigger. What we *really* need is our heavenly Dad himself.

Getting to know him, coming to experience him in our everyday lives, beginning to accept his furious love—it's the most important thing in our lives. It's the ball game. But it's also probably *the* thing most neglected by modern Christians.

It's the *altitude ceiling* through which few of us break.

■ ■ ■

When asked about our primary function as human beings, Jesus responded, "You shall love the Lord your God with all your heart and with all your soul and with all your mind" (Matt. 22:37).

But here's the thing—we can't give what we haven't yet received. We can't love before we've *been* loved. Like those big Titan II rockets, we need to be filled with the rocket fuel of God's love before we can love the way we're meant to. Or like an airplane that'll never fly above its altitude ceiling without some new way to create thrust, we'll never live the lives we're meant to live without being fueled, first, by God's outrageous love.

Receiving love. Being loved. It's the beginning of everything. It's the beginning of life. It's the beginning of *us*. To belong, to be cherished, it's what we need most—even the smartest, even the toughest of men. And only God can address the totality of our needs. Only *he* can fill us with enough love.

So, clearly, we aren't wired for some vague kind of spirituality. We aren't wired for mere rules and lists and sermons. A cold, mechanistic, intellectual faith will never do. Only relationship, conversation, listening and speaking, knowing and following the God of heaven—our head-over-heels, up-in-our-business Father God—can ever fill us with the rocket fuel we need.

By getting in close, by allowing ourselves to be loved up close—that's how we change, grow, mature. By getting to know God, enjoying his presence, trusting him, following him—that's how we become the men we are meant to become. That's how we break through these ceilings that are holding us back. That's how we push the outer edges of the envelopes of our lives.

Here's the truth: in his love we don't stand a chance. His grace and power are simply too powerful. When we move in close, we can't help but change and grow and mature. When we come into his presence, his grace and power permeate every part of our lives.

And then, finally, we're able to begin to discover wholeness and confidence—fearlessness even. We learn how to stop hurting people so much—and hurting ourselves. We begin to discover the joy and peace and purpose and significance and connection we long for—and have tended to look for everywhere else.

When we accept God's love, we get up in the mornings with more enthusiasm and energy and joy. We walk through our days with more confidence and well-being, with a sense of being cared for and provided for, with a sense of belonging and purpose. And we go to bed with more contentment and peace. We're able to relax, finally. And finally, in his love, we're able to begin feeling good about ourselves.

Knowing God and accepting his love strengthens us, lessens fear, gives us energy and focus. It makes us better equipped to deal with hardship and struggle and failure. It makes us more robust, more durable men—able to take on what we never could have in our fragile, depleted, didn't-know-we-were-loved states.

And God's love starts to pour out of us, just as it did from those earliest followers of Jesus. "They turned the world upside down because their hearts had been turned right side up," wrote Billy Graham, that space-age megapastor.[27]

■ ■ ■

We can't stop God from loving us. He does. It's true. It's a thing. And it's always been his plan. He *is* a good, good Father—perfect and loving. And in that love, he created us *to be loved*. As his own precious sons.

You might be asking … But what about those things I've done? Those things I *do*?

What about my sin?

That's a really important question. And one we've got to get sorted if we want to go any further. So that's what we are going to do in chapter 4.

(Spoiler alert: You're about to hear some *very* good news.) So work through the exercises below and keep reading.

■ ■ ■

— ON BOARD —

"BELOVED"

003

God has so much for you. There's so much he wants to share with you. But to receive it, you're going to have to open your heart. You need to let him in.

His love is more than we could ever imagine—and so much more than we could hope to ever enjoy in a human lifetime. But *we* control how much we receive. And if we hope to ever break through these altitude ceilings that keep us stuck, mired in less-than-we'd-like lives, we've got to learn how to receive more.

Consider these questions and capture your responses.

003.1 How do you know God? Is his personality hard or soft? Is he full time or part time? Does he know you? Does he know you *well* or just a little? Is he proud of you or sometimes disappointed? Does he love you easily, or does he tolerate you? Does he *like* you?

Is he a disciplinarian? A judge? Are his expectations of you high or low? Is he here with you now and always? Or is he busy elsewhere? What's he most interested in? Your morality, your performance, your obedience, your sacrifice? Or is he mostly and simply interested in *you*—your heart, your fears, *you*—in just being with *you*?

Pull out a pen or pencil or your phone. Write a few sentences that honestly describe how you view God.

003.2 Circle a number below to indicate how much you believe God loves you:

<< Not so much - ***So*** much >>

1 2 3 4 5 6 7 8 9 10

And pick a number to indicate how much you believe God is interested in you:

<< Not very - ***Very*** interested >>

1 2 3 4 5 6 7 8 9 10

003.3 Brennan Manning, in his book *The Furious Longing of God*, asked his readers whether their relationships with God are characterized by "simplicity, childlike candor, boundless trust, and easy familiarity."[28] I ask you the same question now: Is your relationship characterized by those things? Or is it characterized by complexity, grown-up cynicism, "prove it" distrust, and an easier-to-just-avoid-him attitude?

Or is it somewhere in between?

Write a few sentences accurately describing your relationship with God.

003.4 Are you optimistic about the possibility of establishing a personal relationship with him? About being able to figure out how this relationship stuff works?

Circle a number below to indicate your (honest) level of confidence:

<< Not optimistic at all - - - - - - - - - - - - - - - - Pretty optimistic >>

1 2 3 4 5 6 7 8 9 10

003.5 Spend a few minutes considering your past. Can you bring to mind an occasion or two (or more) when God *was* a father to you? When you felt as if he heard you, saw you, answered your prayers? Describe any times when you experienced peace or joy or help from him—either directly or through other people, events, or circumstances. And if you struggle, ask the Holy Spirit to help you remember.

Surrender to thankfulness as you record these moments of his goodness and fathering—as you dwell on what he's done in your life.

Pray right now:

> *God, I want to know you. The* ***real*** *you. And I want to know myself too—especially who I am to you. I want to understand, as much as I can, just how much you love me. And I want to love you back, more than I do. I want a relationship with you. One that's personal—deep, real, heartfelt, and conversational—even in the midst of this hectic life.*
>
> *But I'm not sure I know how to do or discover any of this, so please come. Help me. Guide me. Teach me. Father me.*
>
> *I need you.*
>
> *Amen.*

Experiment with Lectio Divina. *Lectio Divina* is a Latin phrase meaning "holy reading."[29] It refers to a spiritual practice that traces to third-century Christian methods of connecting with God (and his wisdom) through reading and meditating on verses from the Bible. These methods evolved and improved over the centuries in the monasteries of Europe, and they solidified into a form many Christians use today. When we practice Lectio Divina, we engage Scripture in order to enter into a personal conversation with God.

So find a place where you won't be interrupted for thirty minutes. Start by simply enjoying a few minutes of peace and quiet. And whenever you're ready, read John 13:1–5 (below). Read slowly. Slower than usual, more carefully.

> Before the Feast of the Passover, when Jesus knew that his hour had come to depart out of this world to the Father, having loved his own who were in the world, he loved them to the end. During supper, when the devil had already put it into the heart of Judas Iscariot, Simon's son, to betray him, Jesus, knowing that the Father had given all things into his hands, and that he had come from God and was going back to God, rose from supper. He laid aside his outer garments, and taking a towel, tied it around his waist. Then he poured water into a basin and began to wash the disciples' feet and to wipe them with the towel that was wrapped around him.

Now, after a couple of moments of silence, read the passage a second time. But this time, engage your imagination. Put yourself into the scene. Imagine you're one of the disciples present at the supper. Imagine what Jesus looks like. Imagine the sounds, the physical sensations, the emotions. Try to *feel* what a disciple might have felt.

After a couple more moments of silence, read the passage for a third and final time. This time, as you read, look for words or phrases that catch your attention. When something strikes you, stop reading and focus in. Consider just the words or phrases that stood out. Examine them. Linger over them. Repeat them to yourself. Consider their meanings, the sentiments behind them. Take five minutes for this, at least.

Now, take another five to ten minutes to consider what God might be up to with you, through these feelings or perceptions, these words or phrases. What could he be trying to teach you? How might he be trying to love you through his Spirit? How is he speaking to your heart?

And then, when you're ready, simply respond. Pray. Answer his questions, if you sensed any. Or tell him how you feel or what you think about what you sensed. Or tell him what you think of *him*. Or just say "Thank you." Or ask him questions. Or for his interpretation. Or for guidance. Or forgiveness. Just get honest.

And when you're done praying, don't do anything. Don't move. Don't talk. Don't pray about anything else. Just sit in silence in the presence of the Holy Spirit. Just embrace the closeness of God—enjoy it. Relax and appreciate a few moments of doing nothing except being with your heavenly Dad.

IRON AND BURNT RUBBER AND FORGIVENESS

A twin-engine Convair CV-440 approaches the Cape from the east. The gleaming metal and red and blue stripes stun against the cloudless blue stretching over Florida's Atlantic coast. The fifty-two-seat airliner banks south and comes in low over the beach and Highway A1A.

About a quarter full, the flight originated at Virginia's Langley Air Force Base. It touches down one thousand feet inland at Patrick Air Force Base—back wheels first, then the nose. Patrick AFB occupies the width of a barrier island, one that sits between the ocean (to the east) and tidal flats, salt marshes, and mangrove swamps (to the west). Cocoa Beach is north. Satellite Beach is south.

The airplane rolls to a stop. When the roar and rumble die, after the props slow to a stop, a crew member opens the passenger door and extends the airstairs.

Included on the manifest are two men. They don't know each other and couldn't be more different. As they emerge into the sunlight, mixed in with other passengers, both have the military bearing and cropped haircuts of fighter pilots. But the physical similarities end there.

The first man comes down the stairs as if he owns the place. His eyes smile even when he's not smiling. He wears a short-sleeved shirt that's way more country club than military base.

The second man is in a crisp white button-down shirt and a nifty black tie. His eyes are sad—but more serious than sad. He looks as if he's carrying great responsibility.

Button-Down also looks a bit lost. He scans the tarmac, unable to find whatever he's looking for. What he does see, though, is a righteous blue Corvette—just beyond the tip of the portside wing. And even more startling, a young airman jumps out of the car, snaps a salute to Short Sleeves, and holds the door open.

Turning his attention to more immediate concerns, Button-Down descends and tramps over to the base operations building to retrieve his bag. Once he's got it, he exits the terminal toward the parking lot, hoping to figure out alternate transport because his contact has apparently flaked. He needs to get only about fifteen miles north to America's spaceport. To Cape Canaveral Air Force Station—the launch site for the Mercury missions, the Gemini missions, and the first bunch of Apollo missions. But he's got to find a ride.

Just then: *rugaruga-rugaruga-rugaruga-rugaruga …*

"C'mon, I bet you're going to the Cape."[1]

The man turns and looks up.

It's Short Sleeves, now with aviator sunglasses on, hollering over the sound of his Corvette. "Climb aboard."[2]

A bit confused but grateful, Button-Down nods. He double-times it over, says a slightly awkward "I really appreciate it," stows his bag in the trunk, and slides down into the passenger seat.

As soon as the door clacks shut, they're off. The car peels around 180 degrees, tires smoking, then accelerates northeast—around the terminal and back down the runway!

Short Sleeves clearly has "no concern about being pulled over by the Air Police for speeding and breaking every regulation in the book."[3] Button-Down grips his white leather seat and holds tight. They make a series of gnarly turns. The lefts smash him into the passenger door. He fights the rights so his elbow doesn't end up in the driver's lap.

They speed to the base's gate. An air force policeman salutes too and waves Short Sleeves right through.

Tires smoking again, they make a hard left onto Highway A1A—and they're bookin' at ninety miles per hour in no time.

Short Sleeves erupts. "Eeeee hah."[4]

He then turns, somehow gracefully in the tight space, and extends his hand.

"Hi, I'm Gordo Cooper."[5]

■ ■ ■

The passenger in that Corvette was Gene Kranz. He arrived in Florida in 1960 to join NASA's spaceflight operations team. He would in time become a legend of mission control. He wrote that he "thought of that handshake often in the many years that followed."[6] "Mercury worked," Kranz recounted, "because of the raw courage of a handful of men like Cooper, who sat in heavy metal eggcups jammed on the top of rockets."[7]

Cooper got the opportunity to sit atop two—an Atlas, which pushed the Mercury-Atlas 9 mission into space, and a Titan II, which carried Gemini V. Both missions were tests of endurance. Mercury-Atlas 9 was NASA's first spaceflight lasting longer than twenty-four hours. Gemini V, which Cooper flew with Pete Conrad, was the first time NASA put men into space for the length of time it would take to make a trip to the moon and back.

Gordon Cooper (Foreground) and Pete Conrad in Their Gemini V Spacecraft Moments Before the Hatches Close

Cooper was born to the low, sandstone hills of Shawnee, Oklahoma. His grandfather—who traveled all over Oklahoma, Arkansas, and Texas, preaching about Jesus—"early on" inspired his grandson to read the Bible.[8] He instilled in young Cooper the importance of faith.

> When I was ten years old, I had joined St. Paul's Methodist Church in my hometown.... At the time this had been no weighty decision for me to make or the result of any sudden revelation—it was just something I wanted to do.[9]

He began flying early too. He was twelve when he first soloed in his family's Command-Aire biplane. Cooper was also a Boy Scout, played football, and ran track at the local high school.

World War II was winding down when he graduated from high school in 1945. He enlisted as soon as he could, but the war ended before he could make it overseas. After a few intermediate stops, Cooper ended up at the University of Hawaii. He studied civil engineering and met a woman named Trudy Olson. She was a pilot too—and a Christian.[10] They married in August 1947 and had two daughters.

Cooper was active in the Reserve Officers' Training Corps in college but ended up leaving for the US Air Force before graduating. His first post was Neubiberg Air Force Base near Munich, Germany. He was there for four years. He flew fighters like the F-84 Thunderjet and F-86 Sabre and became commander of the 525th Fighter Bomber Squadron.

Eventually, like so many like him, Cooper made his way to the high desert of California, to Edwards Air Force Base, and became a test pilot. And that's where he got a call from NASA to come to Washington, DC. Some folks there wanted him to consider becoming an astronaut. Over the next few months, he and all the other candidates were subjected to various physical and psychological tests. They were "isolated, vibrated, whirled, heated, frozen, fatigued, and run to high altitude."[11]

When Cooper finished evaluations, he went back to Edwards so confident that NASA would select him, he told his boss "to start looking for a replacement" and alerted his family "to be ready to move."[12]

Cooper was a man of contradictions. He was confident but quiet and gentle too. He was very smart but spoke in what some called a "hillbilly" drawl.[13] He was probably the biggest adrenaline junkie of the early astronaut corps. (He loved racing stock cars and speedboats.) But he was "far more laid back than his peers."[14]

He also had a hard time with the NASA brass. For example, hacked off about a change made to his flight suit just one day before his Mercury flight, he let everyone know by doing a "*very* low flyover" of the NASA administration building. He and his jet fighter "scared the juice out of a number of NASA officials."[15]

Chris Kraft, NASA's first flight director (and Gene Kranz's predecessor), described the scene from his vantage:

> Walt … and I were in his office at the Cape one Sunday afternoon.… We were talking with each other, and a sudden roar came upon us. The roar was a jet airplane diving onto the Cape at a very high rate of speed, which was forbidden. We looked out the window to see none other than Gordo and his F101.[16]

Underneath that rebellious streak, though, was a stronger one—a religious one. Astronaut Cooper maintained strong faith from his youth. In fact, looking back on the naming of his capsule—which all the Mercury astronauts got to do—he said this: "I selected the name *Faith 7* to show my faith in my fellow workers, my faith in all the hardware so carefully tested, my faith in myself, and my faith in God."[17]

And it was on the fourteenth orbit of his Mercury flight that Cooper talked to that God directly.

Here's how a recording device in the capsule captured it:

Cooper: *"Father, thank You, for the success we have had in flying this flight. Thank You for the privilege of being able to be in this position, to be up in this wondrous place, seeing all these many startling, wondrous things that You've created.*

"Help guide and direct all of us that we may shape our lives to be good, that we may be much better Christians, learn to help one another, to work with one another, rather than to fight. Help us to complete this mission successfully. Help us in our future space endeavors that we may show the world that a democracy really can compete, and still is able to do things in a big way, is able to do research, development, and can conduct various scientific, very technical programs in a completely peaceful environment.

"Be with all our families. Give them guidance and encouragement, and let them know that everything will be okay.

"We ask in Thy name.

"Amen."[18]

The prayer "just flowed out," Cooper said.[19] He spoke it "not over the radio for the world to hear but into a small tape recorder"—because he intended it just for his Father God.[20] The world did find out about it, though, when flight transcripts became public and he was asked to read it before a joint session of Congress.

It "doesn't stand as a significant prayer in design quality," Cooper said, "but it was my prayer, and I meant it."[21]

■ ■ ■

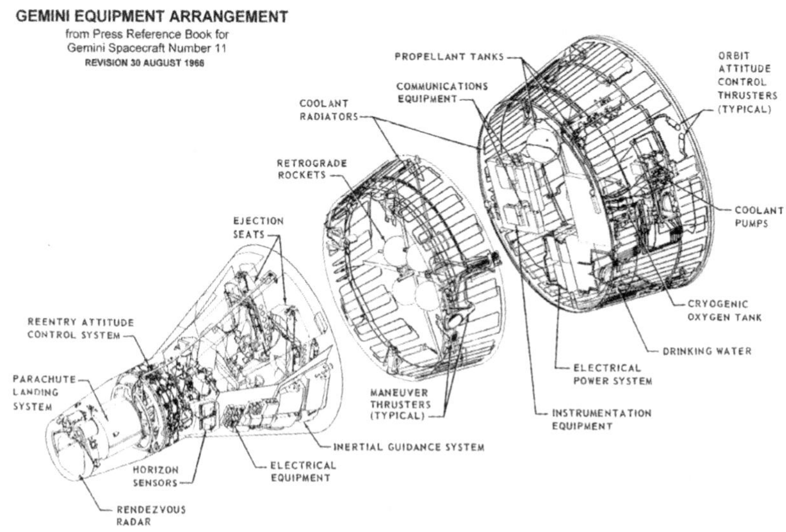

MCDONNELL

A Schematic of the Gemini Capsule

QUESTiON:

"DON'T I NEED TO BE FIXED UP?"

You may have asked ... But what about my sin? How could God want a personal relationship with me? He knows my past. He knows what I'm struggling with right now. How could he ever want to be around someone like ***me****?*

You may have asked ... Shouldn't I come back later, after I get myself all fixed up?

These are great questions, and the truth will blow your mind. **Think bigger.**

■ ■ ■

The idea that we humans could by ourselves master the cosmos took hold in the nineteenth century. But it *really* got rolling in the twentieth—as eye-popping scientific and technological breakthroughs began to accumulate.

But it wasn't limited to the external world. It began to occur to us, over the same period, we might be able to master *us* too. *Inner us. Outer us.* We began to believe that, given some time, we might be able to perfect ourselves—and our lives.

This ethos thrived in our research universities—in the hard sciences and social sciences. It was embraced by academics and practitioners alike. But it was uniquely and remarkably evident in popular culture.

An 1859 book by a man named Samuel Smiles launched the self-help or personal development genre. His book was a hands-on guide for improving one's life—and one's lot in life. It advocated hard work, perseverance, and self-education.

The book sold well. But the self-help market didn't explode until several decades later. In the mid-twentieth century, books like *How to*

Win Friends and Influence People by Dale Carnegie, *Think and Grow Rich* by Napoleon Hill, and *The Power of Positive Thinking* by Norman Vincent Peale all became bestsellers and cultural influencers.

In his book, Hill captured the message of these (and all) self-help books: "You are the master of your own earthly destiny.... You may influence, direct, and eventually control your own environment, making your life what you want it to be."[22]

And midcentury Americans knew exactly what they wanted life to be.

By 1963, the year Gordo Cooper first blasted into the thermosphere, more than 90 percent of American homes had television sets.[23] But for all those TVs, there were only three channels: NBC. CBS. ABC. And those networks broadcast what people wanted: westerns, game shows, and sitcoms depicting "perfect" nuclear families.

Sunny, spick-and-span housewife mothers. Strong, suit-and-tie breadwinner fathers. Smart, smart-alecky, come-around-in-the-end kids. Perfect people. Perfect families. Perfect lives.

Culture was speaking through pop culture, through books and boxes—boxes in family rooms with names like Magnavox Telerama, Philco Predicta, Raytheon Star-monic, and Zenith Flash-matic.

The message was clear: *Get busy and be perfect.*

And everyone was watching.

■ ■ ■

Be perfect hasn't gone away. Quite the opposite. We've upped the intensity of the signal and created new and cunning methods of delivering the message. One social critic dubbed this moment, our day, the "age of perfectionism."[24]

Mass media still does its job, as do our families and communities. But now social media beams *Be perfect* too. First it shows us, in high-res and high-def, how perfect everyone else is—then it inundates us with advice on how to get there ourselves:

> 5 Hacks for Being Happier and More Productive.
> 10 Quick Tips to Live Your Best Life.
> 101 Powerful Ways to Become a Better Person.
> Just click here.

We've also, of course, modernized what "perfect" looks like. And now it looks like this: rich, successful, hip, happy, slim, fit, loved.

It looks like the right degrees from the right colleges. The right careers with the right titles. The right homes in the right neighborhoods and the right number of kids with their own right accomplishments. The right vacations and the right images on the right social networks.

We've got to be crushing it at work, winning at home—and looking good doing it.

And because any of us can help ourselves into "perfect," anything less than perfect is just unacceptable. If we're ever in pain or ever get stuck, it's no one's fault but ours.

■ ■ ■

The problem is, of course, human beings aren't perfect. Not one.

We struggle. We blow it. We make mistakes and sin. *We all do.* "It's clear enough, isn't it, that we're sinners, every one of us, in the same sinking boat with everybody else?" (Rom. 3:19).[25]

We're flat out *less than perfect.* We struggle with honesty. With integrity. With decency. With patience. With kindness. With self-control. We struggle with pornography and infidelity, alcohol and drugs. We all sin. We do so every day. In ways that are big and obvious, of course. But much more often, in ways that are small and sometimes almost imperceptible.

And if we tallied it all up, if we all made lifetime sins lists—honest lists, complete—they would be, by any measure that matters, indistinguishable from one another. Some would lean toward more socially acceptable sins, for sure. But they would all contain more than enough rebellion and sin to disrupt our relationships with God.

Being a member of the human race means (=) being a member of the sinner class.

But there's no room for that sin—and all those mistakes—in a *be-perfect* culture.

So what do we do?

Well, we do what human instinct has always told us to do:

> They heard the sound of the Lord God walking in the garden in the cool of the day, and the man and his wife hid themselves from the presence of the Lord God among the trees of the garden. (Gen. 3:8)

We hide. We obscure failures. We conceal sin. We fake it—in the desperate hope that no one will ever learn the truth.

■ ■ ■

There's always been an aura of perfection around NASA astronauts—but it was especially bright in the late 1950s and 1960s. The agency's public affairs office worked hard to portray their celebrity astronauts as smart, daring, clean cut, churchgoing family men. And they were … *and they weren't.*

Not one of them was perfect, not even Glenn.

If John Glenn had the reputation of being the most straitlaced of the astronauts, Cooper earned a reputation for occupying a position nearer the other end of the conduct spectrum. He was the youngest of the Mercury Seven and, because of that, once remarked, "I think maybe I have a better chance to have some real good fun in this program."[26]

Gordo Cooper and Wernher von Braun on May 5, 1961, during Mercury-Redstone 3—the First American Spaceflight

Cooper had real good fun on the job—working hard and taking risks, but joking and pulling pranks and stunts too, like his hot-dog flyover.

He also looked for real good fun in his time away from work, in his personal life.

His marriage to Trudy was never super strong or stable. There was marital neglect, which was part and parcel of being an astronaut in those days, because of long hours and frequent travel. But there was also infidelity. Cooper wasn't alone in this among the Mercury Seven, but he broke his marriage vows—during his time at Edwards and perhaps after he went to work for NASA too.[27]

"Leroy Gordon Cooper Jr. is very much a human being," wrote one reporter in 1963.[28] He was broken and capable of terrible things—like the rest of us.

But during his initial astronaut evaluation, when asked by NASA about his home life, Cooper hid. Tom Wolfe wrote this:

> The sound instincts of the career officer led Cooper to respond that his family life, with Trudy and the children, was real fine, terrific; regulation issue. This wasn't likely to bear much checking into, however, inasmuch as Cooper and Trudy were not living in the same house or even in the same latitude. They had separated; Trudy and the children were living down near San Diego, while he remained at Edwards.[29]

Cooper was able to convince Trudy to join him out in the California desert. But it was for appearances only—so that marital discord wouldn't disqualify him in the final rounds of the astronaut selection process. And then, when Cooper *was* selected, Trudy "posed like a pro with the other astronauts' wives."[30]

The Coopers faked it. They hid—and they hoped no one would find out the truth.

■ ■ ■

When *Be perfect* is out there and active, when it's reverberating through a society, it creates a system that requires double lives. It incentivizes us to project the good and cover up the bad—and there's always something to cover up. "If we say we have no sin, we deceive ourselves, and the truth is not in us" (1 John 1:8).

Public smiles and private shame.

Be perfect creates a system whereby we move through our days believing that *we* are different: unlovable, unacceptable. Because, in such a system, other people look great—having hid their failures. *But we sure know about our own.* So we live with lurking fear: if people knew the real us, the less-than-perfect us, the sinful us, they'd cut us off, cast us out. Families. Friends. Society.

Even God.

When parents and pastors and other authority figures are the ones telling us to be perfect, it's easy to attribute *Be perfect* to God. It's a small jump from *Be perfect* as a cultural demand to *Be perfect* as a divine command.

■ ■ ■

In Luke 15, Jesus told a story about a man with two sons (vv. 11–32). The parable of the prodigal son opens with the younger son demanding his inheritance prior to his father's death. The request was unusual. It was insulting and, no doubt, deeply hurtful. He was essentially saying to his father, "I don't need you anymore." "I want to go my own way." Maybe even, "I wish you were dead."

Despite the affront, the father acquiesced. And money in hand, the son headed off to a far country and proceeded to spend it. *All of it.* Things got so bad he took a job feeding slop to pigs. He got "so hungry he would have eaten the corncobs in the pig slop, but no one would give him any" (v. 16).[31]

Destitute and desperate, the son formed a plan. He decided to return home and beg his father to take him back—but not as a son. (He figured his father wouldn't do that, not after what he did.) So his plan was to ask to become a hired hand.

The son made the journey home. And when he was "still a long way off, his father saw him" (v. 20). Jesus painted a picture of a father who'd been scanning the horizon for his son ever since he left.

And what was the father's response? He "felt compassion," Jesus said (v. 20). He "ran and embraced him and kissed him" (v. 20). Robes flying, arms open, the father was overjoyed that his precious boy had come home.

After the bear hug, the son started into his no doubt well-rehearsed speech about maybe becoming a lowly servant: "Father, I have sinned against heaven and before you. I am no longer worthy to be called your son" (v. 21). But the father interrupted him. Without a second thought, the father declared, for all to hear, "You are my *son*."

The father put his robe on the boy's shoulders—signifying that he was indeed a member of the family. He put a ring on his finger—signifying that his son had the full authority of a family member. And he put sandals on his son's feet—signifying that his son *was indeed a son*, not a servant. And then the father arranged a feast—a huge party—to celebrate.

■ ■ ■

God has a problem with sin. A big one. *Absolutely.* But not in the way many of us think. Sin *does* get in the way of our relationships with him. It *does* disrupt the father-son relationship. But the disruption occurs not because God rejects us or turns away from us or anything like that. He doesn't. Ever.

Sin disrupts the father-son relationship because it causes *us* to reject *him*—like the prodigal son did to his earthly father in Jesus' parable.

God made humans in love and for love. And because of his love, he gave us free will. Standing in eternity, he's always known each of us through and through—all the way to the end. He's always known our frailty. Our foolishness. He's always known we would abuse our freedom. He's always known we would rebel and rebel and rebel.

> Like an open book, you watched me grow from
> conception to birth;
> all the stages of my life were spread out before you,
> The days of my life all prepared
> before I'd even lived one day. (Ps. 139:16)[32]

Standing in eternity, God saw what we'd do—and he made us still. He wanted to be in relationship with us still. He loved us still—outrageously.

And he does not change. "I the LORD do not change" (Mal. 3:6).

■ ■ ■

In the garden, Adam was exactly whom God wanted him to be—perfectly. "God looked over everything he had made; it was so good, so very good!" (Gen. 1:31).[33] And their father-son relationship was perfect—unmarred by sin and shame and separation.

God and Adam walked and talked and did life together.

But then sin did enter the story. The serpent, Satan, coaxed and cajoled Adam and Eve into rebellion (Gen. 3:1–6). He questioned God's goodness and love. He suggested another way. A way apart from God's way. And when Adam chose it, everything changed.

Perfection was lost.

And that loss became our loss. Somehow Adam's rebellion became ours too. "By the one man's disobedience the many were made sinners" (Rom. 5:19).

Can you feel it? That pull inside to go your own way? To do your own thing?

Like Adam, we're tempted to rebel against God. We're tempted to choose our own ways (our sin) over God's ways; selfishness over generosity; judgment over mercy; independence over relationship. And all of us, even though we might love God very much, give in to those temptations sometimes in varying degrees.

That's why Paul lamented, "What I don't understand about myself is that I decide one way, but then I act another, doing things I absolutely despise" (Rom. 7:15).[34]

It's how Cooper could say, "It just seems as if all my life I have known Christ and wanted to serve Him."[35] Yet he could go and blow up his marriage and betray and hurt the people he loved most.

Sin is a part of our nature. Rebellion is in us. And we can't get free of it. Sin has us trapped. Like a capsule with no hatch. John Eldredge and Brent Curtis, the two-man team who wrote *The Sacred Romance*, described it as being held in "dungeons of darkness."[36] The Bible calls it being locked up in "sin's prison" (Rom. 7:14).[37]

Because of his sin, Adam could no longer be perfectly whom God wanted him to be; neither can we. And Adam's relationship with God ceased to be perfect; so do ours. But God isn't surprised by any of it. Amazingly, he isn't put off.

"God is a forgiving God," Cooper said to the congregation at First Methodist Church in Seabrook, Texas. First Methodist was his home church, and he accepted an invitation to give a sermon there in 1965. God "knows we are human," he told those gathered, "that we err."[38]

Having made us, God knows what we are. And he loves what we are—*as we are*, not just as we "should" be or could be. Even when we struggle to love him back, God is still in love with each of us. His love is never conditional on our actions.

Like the father in Jesus' parable, God loves his sons and daughters because they are his, because they exist, never because of anything they do.

God loves like the best human father, only much, much better. Perfectly. Infinitely.

He grieves our rebellion, of course. He despises the sin that plagues us. He laments the bad choices we make. He detests the separation we choose. But he doesn't turn away. He doesn't reject us for it. No, he turns *toward*. He sympathizes with our humanity—and offers something better than hiding. He doesn't recoil; he leans in and offers help.

"It's a wonder God didn't lose his temper and do away with the whole lot of us. Instead, immense in mercy and with an incredible love, he embraced us" (Eph. 2:3–4).[39] He came into our physical world as a physical man. He did what we couldn't. He *was* perfect. Jesus came and lived among us and "committed no sin" (1 Pet. 2:22).

And then he did something astonishing. He turned it all around.

Jesus somehow drew every last bit of our rebellion and sin into one place, into himself. He bore it all—past, present, future rebellion and sin. And when he died on that cross, all of *it* died too. He dealt with our sin. *All of it. For all time.*

"God so loved the world, that he gave his only Son" (John 3:16). He sent the best of heaven into our broken world to break us out of sin's prison. To break us free of sin and shame. "God didn't go to all the trouble of sending his Son merely to point an accusing finger, telling the world how bad it was. He came to help, to put the world right again" (John 3:17).[40]

Jesus died and rose again not only *for* us but also *as* us. Just as Adam represented the entire human race in failure and rebellion, Jesus represented us in victory and restoration—"by the one man's obedience the many will be made righteous" (Rom. 5:19).

And this was always God's plan, which he formed "before the foundation of the world" (Eph. 1:4). He always knew we would rebel. He knew we would get into trouble. And he always planned to come for us, to rescue and restore us.

God did it (does it) for the same reasons any good human father would rescue a son or daughter from something dangerous or harmful. He does it because he doesn't want us to be in a place of pain and separation. But he also does it because he can't stand the idea of eternity—or even this life—without us. *Without you.*

He wants us to be united with him. God wants to be our father; he wants us to be his beloved sons. And when we break the father-son relationship, when we rebel against it, he comes after us. So that if we want to, we can be reunited.

Immanuel. "God with us." *Abba.* "Papa."

■ ■ ■

Jesus' victory over sin becomes our victory when we decide to let him into our lives—when we decide to follow him. When we do that,

Jesus reengineers us: "If anyone is in Christ, he is a new creation" (2 Cor. 5:17).

What Jesus did on the cross allows us to transform, over time, and become more and more like what Adam was before the fall—perfectly whom God wants us to be and in perfect relationship with him, without sin, without shame, without separation.

But we don't become perfect in an instant, of course. We don't instantly become the men God wants us to be. And we don't come back into perfect relationship with him in an instant either.

What does happen, though, is that we become *able*. We become *able to become* those men. Able to be taught and trained to deal with sin. Able to be taught and trained to confess and repent, to live in freedom and joy and peace and purpose. Able to be taught and trained to be in relationship and conversation with our head-over-heels Father God.

Able to come home.

We'll continue to struggle, of course, but less and less. We'll heal and learn and be less and less tempted by sin—more able to recognize temptations for what they are.

We *will* become perfectly whom God wants us to be—but slowly. And not completely until Jesus returns and makes "all things new" (Rev. 21:5).

Until then, he transforms us "from glory to glory" (2 Cor. 3:18).[41]

■ ■ ■

But we cannot *become* alone. We cannot become the men we want to be—or whom God wants us to be—by ourselves. We cannot mature and become whole alone. And we cannot, by ourselves, restore our relationships with God. No amount of planning or preparation, sheer will or self-discipline or sin avoidance will get us there.

Having made us, only God knows how to help us *become*. Only he knows how to make us perfect. Only he knows the process, the right words to say. Only he knows where we need to go—what we need to go through. Only he knows what we need to face—what we need to experience.

Only God knows how to motivate us without wounding us. Only he knows how to heal what needs healing. Only he knows how to deal with our old tendencies, our neuroses, our bad habits, our coping strategies, our attachments and addictions, our wrong beliefs and bad interpretations.

So, *becoming* happens by *being together*. It happens with contact. It happens by encounter. It happens by experience. And the more we're with him, the more it happens.

So here's the upshot: we've simply got to learn to show up in our sin and shame. We must be willing to come into contact with God while we're still broken and ashamed.

And then we need to stay. And keep staying. Even when shame tells us to run and hide.

The order is crucial. *Be with* comes before *become*. We'd like it to be flipped, for sure. We'd like to be able to get perfect on our own. As Brennan Manning wrote, "Push, pull, click, click, one saint that quick."[42] That would be nice. We could get ourselves all fixed up and then approach God—without sin, without shame.

But it doesn't work like that. If we try to flip the order, nothing happens. (I've tried.)

"Let us then with confidence draw near to the throne of grace, that we may receive mercy and find grace to help in time of need" (Heb. 4:16).

Nothing happens because *grace* is precisely what we need and don't have. "Grace," wrote the great disentangler Dallas Willard, "is God acting in our lives to accomplish what we can't accomplish on our own."[43] We need grace to change. We need grace to *become*. Without it, we can't escape the dark dungeons of sin. That's why Paul wrote,

> I've tried everything and nothing helps. I'm at the end of my rope. Is there no one who can do anything for me? Isn't that the real question?

> The answer, thank God, is that Jesus Christ can and does. He acted to set things right in this life of contradictions where I want to serve God with all my heart and mind, but am pulled by the influence of sin to do something totally different. (Rom. 7:24–25)[44]

God says, "Come as you are, and get better *with me*, in my love." And when we go to him like that, he pours grace into our lives. He heals what's hurt. He cleans us up. But he does it for real—not the fake way the Coopers tried to sanitize their image for NASA. Or the way we try to scrub up our public images by hiding what we're ashamed of.

God actually deals with our sin. And he doesn't sweep any of it under the rug.

■ ■ ■

But, of course, it's not always easy going to God. We live in a physical world—a world of time and space, cause and effect, where bad behavior is met with bad consequences. Our world deals harshly with *less than perfect*. And because we expect harsh treatment whenever we're exposed for who we truly are, we often expect harsh treatment from God too.

We reason that, because of our mistakes and our sins, God just *must* love us less, *like* us less. Our sin *must* make him want to be in relationship with us less.

So we tend to take a physical-world approach, a time-and-space approach—just as Adam and Eve did in Genesis 3. When we fail yet again, we tend to want to hide, to withdraw from God for a time. We avoid him until we feel better about ourselves, until enough time has passed since our last transgression, or until we've done some "good" things to offset our bad behavior.

Only then are we willing to go back.

But this creates relationships characterized by oscillation—by movement back and forth —by coming and going, coming and going. This approach is intuitive to our physical natures. It comes naturally. (It did to me.) But here's the problem: it cuts us off from God right when we need him most. It cuts us off from the source of forgiveness and healing and guidance right when we need them most.

No wonder we're struggling with those same old sins.

■ ■ ■

Resisting this urge to come and go is difficult for me. God's definitely expanded my understanding of the depth, breadth, and nature of his love, but I still struggle with it.

The most dramatic expansion happened four years ago, when God invited me into a journey. It was a series of short trips actually, physical trips, combined with an inner journey. The journey consisted of hundreds of experiences—a few jaw dropping, many less than that, but all demonstrating his astonishing love.

A visit to McMinnville, Oregon, kicked it off. Jenn and I met and prayed with a sage and selfless pastor there. (That was when I recalled that twelve-year-old "God must love me less" pronouncement.) The journey included that hunting trip to Montana, as well as a fly-fishing trip with a friend to the Shasta Cascade region of California. And it concluded with a retreat in the Rockies.

The whole thing lasted about half a year.

But it was after all that, after that six-month period, that my fight with *come and go* began in earnest. While I did indeed have a better picture of how much God loves his sons and daughters, my stubborn sense of justice still demanded I withdraw from him whenever I'd fall back into some stubborn sin. To make sense of all that love, I think I was trying somehow to compel it to be conditional—contingent on my behavior.

Given the struggle, I began to wonder whether I might extend the interior, spiritual portion of my Oregon/Montana/Colorado journey by a few months—because I wanted to experiment a bit. And I did. And whenever I'd blow it one more time—like with harsh and impatient outbursts toward one of the members of my immediate family—I'd force myself into his presence. (And with three teenage kids in our house, there were lots of opportunities for experimentation.)

It was the opposite of what I wanted to do, but I would run to God. I would go and listen to music and worship him. I would get in touch with friends and confess my failures. I would pray and listen for his voice. Sometimes I'd pray and listen even in the moment—in the very moment of realizing that I was doing it yet again!

And my understanding of God's love expanded way further. My relationship with him went way higher. I broke through what had been, for me, an altitude ceiling.

■ ■ ■

God doesn't act according to human justice or human fairness. He isn't governed by any laws of the natural world. He does his own thing—and it "surpasses knowledge" (Eph. 3:19). Unconditional, unchanging, unending love is just too hard for our human minds to imagine. It is radical. It is outrageous. It's a sacred mystery.

And we're going to have to start getting comfortable with that kind of mystery. Because we need his love and grace—even when we don't feel we deserve them. And we're going to need to learn to meet his doesn't-make-sense actions with a doesn't-make-sense act of our own, which is simply to say … "Okay."

The younger son in Jesus' parable didn't wait to pull himself together before returning. He showed up smelling of the road, maybe still of slop and pig filth. He expected rejection, justice. But he needed help; he was desperate. So he went home to his dad, just as he was. And what he got was unconditional love. Instead of corncobs, he got a feast.

Despite significant personal failures, despite sin, Cooper found his way back to God too—because he knew that he needed him. And he knew that God would accept him. That he would be there, no matter what. On the ground *and* in outer space. "I felt as if I needed Him just as much 150 miles above the earth as I need Him every day," Cooper said.[45]

■ ■ ■

In his sermon at Seabrook Methodist, Cooper preached about God's forgiveness. When we come to God, when we come out of hiding, Cooper explained, "He will forgive us and give us the strength and guidance we need." "This," he said, "is the true meaning of faith."[46]

We tend to think being a Christian—being a saint—is about how little we sin. It isn't, not really. We think how much or how little we sin is what God cares about most. It's not.

"A saint," described Thomas Merton, twentieth-century mystic and monk, "is not someone who is good but who experiences the goodness of God."[47]

What God cares about most is that we show up. What he wants most is that we encounter him, experience him, get to know him. *Because he trusts himself.* When he sees us come out of hiding, he breathes a God-sized sigh of relief, because he knows the power of his love and grace and goodness in our lives.

He knows that when we're with him, nothing can take us down—not sin, nothing.

■ ■ ■

That's what the God of heaven is like. And if you want it, you too can have a personal relationship with him. Anyone can. Now, *that's* good news.

So do you? Do you want it?

If so, chapter 5 is all about *how*. It's about how we build relationships with him—even in this crazy modern world.

■ ■ ■

— ON BOARD —

"FORGIVEN"

004

If you want a real and close relationship with God and if you want to become the man you're meant to be, you've got to be okay with showing up in your less-than-perfect-ness. You've got to be willing to go into the presence of our loving Father God. In prayer. In study. In solitude. In service. In worship. In community. In celebration. All the time, as much as you can. Right after—or even better, *during*—your rebellion. Even when your sinful mistakes are happening right now!

You've got to learn to trust his goodness and trust him to change you—more than you trust yourself. Much more.

Consider these questions and capture your responses.

004.1 Have you ever received the *Be perfect* message? Have you ever felt as if standards are really high and as if you aren't measuring up?

Take out a pen or pencil or your phone, and compose a few sentences that describe your experience with *Be perfect.*

004.2 Make a bulleted list of all the things that can complete this sentence: For me, "perfect" has looked like ____________________.

Be specific. Be vulnerable. Here are some hints:*

---

* Just to be clear, these things aren't bad in and of themselves. The problem arises when we set up rules for ourselves and measure our self-worth according to whether we follow them. Jesus set us free, even from laws like these: "For freedom Christ has set us free; stand firm therefore, and do not submit again to a yoke of slavery" (Gal. 5:1).

- having a certain amount of money in my bank account
- performing at a certain level at work
- living in the house I want
- taking cool vacations
- being thin, physically fit
- having a great relationship with my spouse
- having kids who are performing at a certain level in school or in sports

004.3 Do you identify with the younger son in Jesus' parable of the prodigal son? Do you ever feel the urge to turn away from God's love? Do you ever feel like cutting your own path or taking a path offered by culture? Nouwen wrote, "I am the prodigal son every time I search for unconditional love where it cannot be found. Why do I keep ignoring the place of true love and persist in looking for it elsewhere? Why do I keep leaving home where I am called a child of God, the Beloved of my Father?"[48]

Circle a number below to indicate how much you identify with the younger son:

<< NOT SO MUCH - *SO* MUCH >>

1 2 3 4 5 6 7 8 9 10

Write a few sentences about a time when you took the prodigal road.

004.4 Have you ever tried to obscure failures? Have you ever tried to conceal sin from your family, your friends, your communities?

Write a few sentences that describe a time when you tried to do this.

004.5 Are you surprised by this new approach to holiness offered in this chapter? Are you surprised to hear that God doesn't turn away from you when you fail but that he turns toward you with compassion and understanding—that he *leans in* to help?

<< NOT SO MUCH - VERY SURPRISED >>

1 2 3 4 5 6 7 8 9 10

Pray right now:

Father, I see you dropping everything and running toward me, arms outstretched, your face full of joy and love. I know you hate it when I rebel and separate myself from you—but also know you celebrate like crazy when I return. I love how you accept me, love me, and throw a party for me, no matter where I've been or what I've done.

But, I confess, these things I've done make me sometimes hesitant to draw near, to be honest with you, to listen to you. But I want to be the kind of man who runs to his Dad anyway, just as my Dad is running toward me. I want to be the kind of man who welcomes his Dad's love when I need it most—not just when I'm feeling good about myself. I want to be the kind of man who gets validation from his Father's love, not from some "perfection" rules I (or someone else) created.

I want to be the kind of man who walks right into his Father's feast—even when I don't feel as if I deserve to be enjoying a party. I want to be the kind of man who's always desperate for his Dad's love, even when I don't feel worthy of it.

And thank you, thank you, Jesus, for making all this possible.

Amen.

Confess your sins to God, repent, and be forgiven—fully. Spend thirty minutes or so making a list of things you've never confessed to God. While painful, this exercise is always good. It's the only way to replace shame with freedom and love and acceptance. "If we confess our sins, he is faithful and just to forgive us our sins and to cleanse us from all unrighteousness" (1 John 1:9). And "as far as the east is from the west, so far does he remove our transgressions from us" (Ps. 103:12).

So make your list as complete as possible. Take a bit longer than half an hour, if you need it. Hold on to the list overnight, even a few days, if you feel compelled to—allowing more things to come to mind. Then, whenever you're ready, take your list to God. Be honest and read to him the items.*

And when you are done, hear these words, God's response to your confession:** "I will remember their sins and their lawless deeds no more" (Heb. 10:17).

---

* If you feel a divine nudge in your heart, read your list to a trusted friend as well.

** And ask yourself, Can I forgive myself? Because while God forgives instantly, we rarely operate so fast. We can refuse to forgive ourselves for years, decades even, thinking that doing so somehow pleases God. It doesn't. It hurts him further because it hurts us. So if you're having a hard time forgiving yourself, ask him for help. It will come.

And now, repent. If you can do it with a true heart, tell God you want to turn away from your sins. Tell him you want to turn your back on your old self, on the man who did those things. If you're willing, tell him you don't want to be that man anymore. Tell him you want to start fresh, to become a new man.

Worship. When we struggle to accept his mercy and love, instead of trying to *will* ourselves to accept them (because that's hard), it's often easier to flip things. When we engage in a practical act of loving him—like worshipping, for example—we open ourselves to receive *his* love *for us*. Instead of trying to bend our minds toward a theoretical acceptance of his love, we just let him love us. And he's really good at that.

So find a space and a time when you won't be interrupted. Your office. Your bedroom. Your car, maybe. And spend thirty minutes or so playing your favorite worship music,* listening to the lyrics—and singing them, if you're willing. There's nothing quite like hearing your own voice in worship.

---

* If you need suggestions, there are worship playlists handcrafted just for men at www.gatherministries.com/music.

FINISTERRE

The road in the end taking the path the sun had taken,
into the western sea, and the moon rising behind you
as you stood where ground turned to ocean: no way
to your future now but the way your shadow could take,
walking before you across water, going where shadows go,
no way to make sense of a world that wouldn't let you pass
except to call an end to the way you had come,
to take out each frayed letter you had brought
and light their illumined corners; and to read
them as they drifted on the late western light;
to empty your bags; to sort this and to leave that;
to promise what you needed to promise all along,
and to abandon the shoes that brought you here
right at the water's edge, not because you had given up
but because now, you would find a different way to tread,
and because, through it all, part of you would still walk on,
no matter how, over the waves.[49]

// David Whyte, poet

SILICON AND OUTER SPACE AND DARING

It's nearly unfathomable. It's a place countless generations gazed up at and wondered about, but few dreamed we might actually go.

But Frank Borman, Jim Lovell, and Bill Anders have gone there. And they are, just now, coasting silently around the moon in their Apollo command module.

The Mercury capsule was designed for one person, with 36 cubic feet of habitable space.[1] The Gemini capsule was designed for two, with 55 cubic feet.[2] But the Apollo command module is designed for three, and it has a roomy 210 cubic feet of space for the astronauts.[3] And it's this latter craft that has carried these three adventurers here from launch at Kennedy Space Center in Florida. And if all goes as planned, it's what will carry them back to Earth for splashdown in the Pacific.

But because of external frost and internal condensation—and because the men have been busy doing the work of NASA astronauts—none of these guys has gotten a good look at the goal. But Borman, the man at the controls, the commander of this mission, is about to:

> I'll never forget my first glimpse of the moon through the triangular eight-by-eleven window on my side. We had just completed the first turn that put us into orbit when I saw below us the hostile face of the moon. I felt as if *Apollo 8* had been transported into a world of science fiction, with incredible lighting and awesome, forlorn beauty—desolate beyond belief.[4]

The men complete their first orbit, then another, noting all along how beaten up and lifeless the moon looks. With an atmosphere too thin to protect it from meteoroids, the lunar surface is pocked with impact craters. Borman reported, "It's a vast, lonely, forbidding-type existence, or expanse of nothing, that looks rather like clouds and clouds of pumice stone."[5]

The men keep circling and observing the moon's surface—"like explorers from ancient days, seeing a new land for the first time," wrote Gene Kranz.[6]

But then, on their third orbit, through more than an inch of glass,* Borman sees something else—something incredible, almost inexpressible:

> I happened to glance out one of the still-clear windows just at the moment the earth appeared over the lunar horizon. It was the most beautiful, heart-catching sight of my life, one that sent a torrent of nostalgia, of sheer homesickness, surging through me. It was the only thing in space that had any color to it. Everything else was either black or white, but not the earth. It was mostly a soft, peaceful blue, the continents outlined in a pinkish brown. And

* NASA engineers made the Apollo command module windows with double panes of 0.25-inch tempered silica (silicon dioxide) glass and 0.7-inch panes of amorphous fused silicon glass. Silica is a common mineral that forms when stars explode.

> always the white clouds, like long streaks of cotton suspended above that immense globe.[7]

Earthrise, Taken by Bill Anders on the Morning of December 24, 1968

Borman is seeing *home*. Love. Goodness. Family. Friendship. Protection. Care. Comfort.

All of it rising blue and majestic above the forbidding lunar landscape. A "miracle of creation"—our good home hanging alone in the midst of vast, "eternal cold."[8]

But it's so far away. Borman can blot the entire thing from his vision with just his thumb—he can hide all "the dearest things in life" under a single thumbnail.[9]

On their ninth and second-to-last orbit—just before they're to begin their long trip back—the men click on a TV camera and start broadcasting to that indigo and lonely orb. To an audience back home that's both enormous and eager for any word from their brave spacemen. *TV Guide* estimates that one out of four humans will hear their out-of-this-world telecast.[10] Men and women, boy and girls, families and friends, all huddled anxiously around TVs and radios in living rooms and dens and kitchens.

To nearly one billion fellow human beings, across hundreds of thousands of miles of space, the astronauts describe what they see. They take turns giving impressions. Of wonder. Of dread. They pan the camera to show the surface of the moon sweeping by at four thousand miles per hour, a mere sixty miles beneath the command module.

Then, just before signing off, the astronauts offer one final message. They decide to share their "feeling of closeness to the Creator of all things."[11]

Anders: *"For all the people back on Earth, the crew of Apollo 8 has a message that we would like to send to you."*

Anders: *"In the beginning, God created the Heaven and the Earth. And the Earth was without form and void, and darkness was upon the face of the deep. And the spirit of God moved upon the face of the waters, and God said, 'Let there be light.' And there was light. And God saw the light, that it was good, and God divided the light from the darkness."*

Lovell: *"And God called the light Day, and the darkness he called Night. And the evening and the morning were the first day. And God said, 'Let there be a firmament in the midst of the waters. And let it divide the waters from the waters.' And God made the firmament and divided the waters which were under the firmament from the waters which were above the firmament. And it was so. And God called the firmament Heaven. And the evening and the morning were the second day."*

Borman: *"And God said, 'Let the waters under the Heavens be gathered together into one place. And let the dry land appear.' And it was so. And God called the dry land Earth. And the gathering together of the* *waters called he seas. And God saw that it was good. And from the crew of Apollo 8, we close with good night, good luck, a Merry Christmas and God bless all of you—all of you on the good Earth."*

Mission Control: *"That's both biblical and a geological lesson that none of us will forget."*[12]

It's Christmas Eve 1968.

■ ■ ■

Apollo 8 was the first manned mission to the moon. Astronauts Borman, Lovell, and Anders traveled across nearly 240,000 miles of space, reached the moon, orbited it ten times, and returned to Earth.

It would be another 205 days before humans would actually set foot on the moon's surface—with Apollo 11 and Neil Armstrong and Buzz Aldrin. But Apollo 8 was an unbelievable accomplishment. And in terms of daring, it stands alone among all NASA missions, those that came before and even those that followed.

It was "a major leap forward," said Chris Kraft, director of NASA flight operations, "the most important flight of Apollo by far. No comparison."[13]

Apollo 8 was the first time any human left the safety of Earth. It was the first time we broke free of Earth's gravity. "It was … the first time humans didn't experience night and sunrises and sunsets, the first time humans saw Earthrise, the first time humans were exposed to deep-space radiation," marveled Teasel Muir-Harmony, curator at the Smithsonian National Air and Space Museum.[14]

It was the first time any humans struck out into the dark, cold emptiness of space and actually reached another celestial body.

Of all NASA missions, it was the mission into the greatest unknown. By way of comparison, the farthest from Earth any prior mission had gone was Gemini XI—which reached a maximum distance of 850 miles.[15] And going in, some at the space agency pegged the chances of success at about 50 percent.[16]

President Kennedy called the moon shot "the most hazardous and dangerous and greatest adventure on which man has ever embarked."[17] He called the journey to the moon a voyage on a "new ocean," a "new sea."[18] And Borman and Lovell and Anders were the first men to sail on it. Their flight was a triumph of science and mathematics, preparation and procedure, but boldness and courage too.

Apollo 8 is best remembered, though, for the Genesis reading—when the astronauts turned their monumental feat of exploration into a global spiritual moment. The *New York Times* called it "the emotional high point of their fantastic odyssey."[19]

"For us," wrote Gene Kranz, "it would become the second greatest Christmas story ever told. Think about the imagery of a rocket soaring through limitless space, so close to heaven the passengers could reach out and touch the face of God."[20]

And it might never have happened without air force colonel Frank Borman.

Borman was born in Gary, Indiana. But the cold and wet of that rusty city played havoc with his sinuses, so his parents moved the family to the American Southwest—to warm and dry Tucson, Arizona. In Tucson, Borman thrived. He became quarterback of the local high school football team and won a state championship his senior year.

He then went to West Point for college. And after graduation, he joined the US Air Force. He became a fighter pilot with the Forty-Fourth Fighter Bomber Squadron in the Philippines, flying T-33 Shooting Stars and F-84 Thunderjets.

After four years abroad, Borman returned to pursue a graduate degree in aeronautical engineering at Caltech, to teach at West Point, and to become a test pilot at Edwards. Then, in 1962, NASA selected Borman (along with Ed White) to be part of the second group of astronauts—the New Nine.

It didn't take long for Borman to earn respect. He commanded Gemini VII, even though it was his first mission. He flew with Jim Lovell and set a record of fourteen days in orbit, surpassing Gordon

Cooper and Pete Conrad's eight days with Gemini V. And because of the success of that mission, NASA tapped Borman to command Apollo 8, only the second manned space mission after the tragic Apollo 1 fire.

A week before leaving for Kennedy Space Center, Borman attended Sunday services at St. Christopher Episcopal in League City, Texas. The church is close to the Manned Spacecraft Center in Houston, and it's where the Bormans attended church—and where he was scheduled that year to do some Christmas readings.

"We kidded Frank about going to such lengths—all the way to the moon—to get out of taking part in our Christmas Eve services," said the Reverend James Buckner.[21] Another friend piped up. He said the church shouldn't let him off "so easy" and suggested that Borman still read the Scripture—but from space.[22]

And that conversation set off a chain of events that would lead the crew of Apollo 8 to write passages from the first chapter of Genesis right into their NASA flight plans.

Frank Borman Suiting Up on Launch Day, December 21, 1968

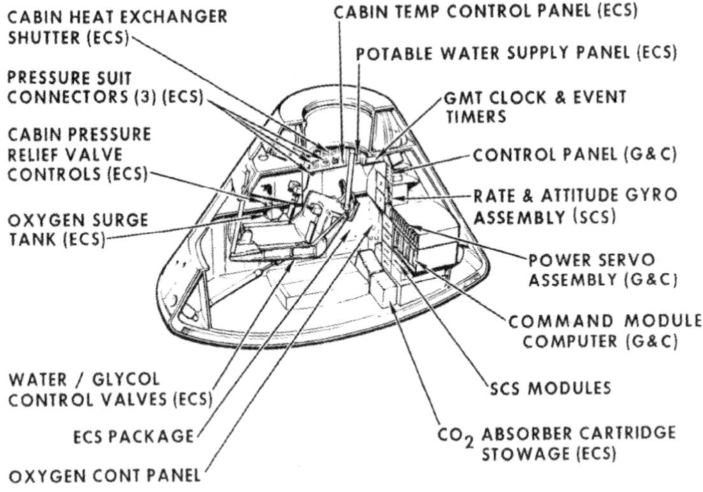

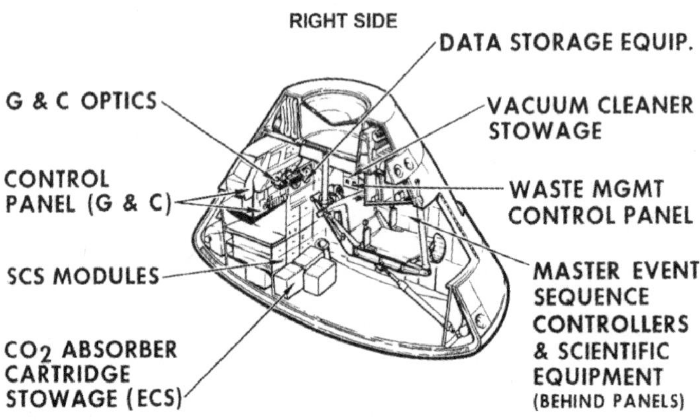

Apollo Command Module Interior

QUESTiON:

"HOW DOES ALL THIS WORK?"

You may have asked … How ***do*** *I encounter God? How* ***do*** *I get to know him personally? How do I experience his power, goodness, love directly? And is it possible to* ***know*** *all this is real?*

You may have asked … How does all this work?

These are great questions, and the truth will blow your mind. **Think bigger.**

■ ■ ■

Christmas Eve 1968 was close to the peak of the space age. Apollo was cranking at high speed. NASA had just sent men to the moon, and the agency was on the cusp of landing them there. It was a heady time. Faith in science and technology was soaring. People were optimistic, growing ever more confident in our abilities to understand ourselves and our universe—and to shape for ourselves a better future.

But it was also a time of cultural upheaval and protest. The war in Vietnam was raging—roughly half of all who would die in the conflict would fall in 1968 and 1969. Martin Luther King Jr. and Robert Kennedy had just been assassinated, and race riots had broken out in more than one hundred American cities.

Young people were rejecting the conformity and traditional values of prior decades. Many Americans were adopting new worldviews and embracing new ideas about what is real and what is right. And that led to breakthroughs in civil rights and gender equality.

But it also shifted how we, as a people, viewed God. More Americans than ever were adopting what one academic called "radical godlessness."[23] British professor of church history Hugh McLeod speculated that this time period "may come to be seen as marking a rupture as profound as that brought about by the Reformation."[24]

And one voice calling for such a rupture was Bertrand Russell. A philosopher, mathematician, and member of the British House of Lords, Russell wrote more than seventy books and won a Nobel Prize in Literature. And his attacks on faith were frequent and vehement, written with style and wit.

Below is an exchange between Russell and an interviewer. It captures the spirit of the age—the spirit sweeping through the United States (and the world) in the late 1960s:

> "Let us suppose, sir, that after you have left this sorry vale, you actually found yourself in heaven, standing before the Throne. There, in all his glory, sat the Lord—not Lord Russell, sir: God."
>
> Russell winced.
>
> "What would you think?"
>
> "I would think I was dreaming."
>
> "But suppose you realized you were not? Suppose that there, before your very eyes, beyond a shadow of a doubt, *was* God. What would you say?"
>
> The pixie wrinkled his nose. "I probably would ask, 'Sir, why did you not give me better evidence?'"[25]

■ ■ ■

We should all want proof of God. We should all desire and strive to encounter and experience him—and accumulate and examine evidence of him.

But we're wrong to demand he produce a certain kind of evidence. And that's what Russell was doing. The question he really wanted to ask was "Why did you not give me better *physical* evidence?"

Russell wanted to subject God to the scientific method. He wanted to put God under a microscope; he wanted to figure him out with a ruler or a scale, a mass spectrometer or a DNA sequencer.

But while the scientific method is a superb method for making discoveries and acquiring knowledge, its usefulness is limited to the natural world. It works in the here and now. It works when phenomena are physically observable and predictable and repeatable.

Jesus taught us, however, that "God is spirit" (John 4:24). He's what theologians call transcendent. He's not limited to a physical body or by the natural world. He "inhabits eternity" (Isa. 57:15). He exists outside the here and now; he exists beyond worldly weights and measures, apart from data, above human understanding. We will *never*, therefore, be able to gauge or get our hands around him with any finite tool or device—or with our finite minds.

Now, God does exist in the here and now too—as discussed in prior chapters. He is also what theologians call immanent. He is "over all and through all and in all" (Eph. 4:6)—and *all* means "all," including the natural world. But he's so fundamental and so powerful that he alone controls when and how he reveals himself to us here in the physical realm—"he does all that he pleases" (Ps. 115:3).

And when he does choose to reveal himself to us, he doesn't do so in ways that we can examine in a laboratory or evaluate with some instrument. He doesn't do so in any ways we can predict or cause him to repeat on demand.

So if we try to use machine-age methods to discover God—to encounter him, to experience him—and come away confused and frustrated and doubting, we haven't proved that God doesn't exist or that he isn't near or interested in us or relevant to our lives or that the spiritual realm isn't real or anything like that.

All we've proved is that we have, once again, tried to use improper instruments and employ wrong methods—like if we tried to use a ruler to measure love or a scale to weigh joy.

■ ■ ■

If we want to encounter and experience God, if we want to accumulate and examine evidence of him, what we need is an instrument and a method that can take into account the whole of reality—not just part of it. What we need is an instrument that's sensitive to both the natural and the supernatural.

And fortunately for us, God has forged just such an instrument. And he's taught us just such a method.

The instrument is among his most stunning. And each of us has one: *the human heart.*

We know *of* God with our minds. We *know* him with our hearts. The latter is what Borman's predecessor at NASA, John Glenn, was talking about when he said, "Although we can't weigh and measure God in scientific terms, we can feel and know Him."[26]

Our brains are designed for knowing facts, for understanding how things work, for grappling with questions of math or science or physics or philosophy or history. But our hearts are made for *feeling*—for experiencing beauty and joy and sorrow, for delighting in mystery and wonder. (Like when that rush of emotion flowed through Borman's heart when he first gazed on Earth from the vicinity of the moon.) And our hearts are also made for that other kind of knowing—knowing people. And they are made for *loving*.

And our hearts work as well in the spiritual realm as they do in the physical world. They are the instruments God designed for us and gave to us so we could encounter him. It is through them that we sense his presence. It's through our heart instruments that we communicate with him. And it is through them that we are able to know him relationally and love him.

God made relationship with him possible by putting "the Spirit of his Son *into our hearts*" (Gal. 4:6, emphasis added). The Holy Spirit, the very Spirit of Jesus, is who makes possible the connection between each one of us and our Father God—the transcendent God of heaven. The Holy Spirit is our transmission link; he makes communication feasible.

God put some of heaven inside you—so you could experience some of heaven now.

■ ■ ■

The primary mission of Apollo 8 was to reach the moon, orbit it, and return safely. But the folks at NASA wanted to make the most out of the unique opportunity. So, secondarily, they hoped to complete some "worthwhile scientific tasks" during the lengthy journey.[27]

Those tasks, they decided, would include photographing the lunar surface and scouting for possible future landing sites. So Borman and his crew took along two Hasselblad 500 EL cameras and a sixteen-millimeter Maurer motion picture camera.[28] They took more than eight hundred still photographs and over seven hundred feet of movie film.[29]

But the moon's surface wasn't the only thing Borman saw. At one of his many postflight press conferences, he told reporters what else he'd seen: "I saw evidence that God lives."[30] He saw evidence out there. And he knew that he knew—God was real.

But he didn't try to snap a photo of God. He knew those cameras he had along weren't the right instruments to encounter him.

The right instrument was his heart. And the data he gathered with it—what he sensed the Holy Spirit whispering to him as he raced through outer space—was every bit as compelling as those breathtaking photographs he and his crew brought back.

A. W. Tozer wrote, "We have in our hearts organs by means of which we can know God as certainly as we know material things through our familiar five senses."[31]

■ ■ ■

Not only do we have the right instruments to encounter the God of heaven; we also know the right method. God has taught us. It's time honored. We, his followers, have been using this particular method to discover him—to encounter him, to experience him—since the time of Abraham because it's the one that makes our heart instruments especially sensitive to his presence and his voice.

The right method? Well, it's to hit the road. To go on an adventure. To head off into the wilderness alone. To embark on a quest. The right method to encounter the God of heaven is to engage in the ancient spiritual practice of *journeying*.

Four thousand years ago, God called Abraham into the unknown: "Go from your country and your kindred and your father's house to the land that I will show you" (Gen. 12:1). And Abraham did. He walked into a vast desert.

> When he left he had no idea where he was going. By an act of faith he lived in the country promised him, lived as a stranger camping in tents.... Abraham did it by keeping his eye on an unseen city with real, eternal foundations—the City designed and built by God. (Heb. 11:8–10)[32]

Jacob met God in the wilderness, wrestling with him by the side of a river (Gen. 32:22–30). Moses met God in the wilderness, several times climbing a mountain alone to encounter him (Ex. 3:1–4; 19:2–3; Deut. 34:1). David met God in the wilderness (Ps. 63). Elijah met God in the wilderness (1 Kings 19:4–9).

Jesus and his followers did too. Jesus went into the wilderness often, when he needed uninterrupted person-to-person contact with his Father (Luke 5:16). Paul, after his conversion on the Damascus Road, went into the desert to meet God. "He went to Arabia," wrote biographer John Pollock, "to learn—from the risen Jesus."[33]

"The Gospels smell of the road," wrote adventurer and academic Charles Foster.[34] And many other followers of Jesus have, for nearly two thousand years, followed in the footsteps of these biblical examples.

With vim and zeal in their hearts, they left what was familiar and comfortable to go on holy adventures, epic quests, sacred pilgrimages. They hiked into the Egyptian desert. They trekked to Rome and Jerusalem. They walked the Camino de Santiago to northern Spain.

Their journeys have lasted weeks, sometimes months, oftentimes years. For almost two millennia, there's been a mighty march, a massive movement of human beings—hearts yearning to encounter the God of heaven.

Because we are made not to be sedentary or stuck or static but *to go*. To roam. We're hardwired to move our muscles, to exercise our minds—and to allow our hearts to be moved by God.

We're made to travel. To see and hear. To touch and taste and smell. We're made to brave wild places. We're made to explore new territories and take risks and face dangers and overcome challenges. We're made to wander and get lost. We are made to climb high and fall and get up and try again.

"Exploration," Borman once said, "is really the essence of the human spirit."[35]

But even deeper than our yearning to explore is our longing to know God. "Our restless and wandering pilgrim hearts," wrote N. T. Wright, "are restless precisely because the loving God has made us for himself."[36] We're made to be in loving relationship with him.

But to love God, we must *know* him first. We cannot love someone whom we do not know—not really, not intimately. And when Jesus talked about that kind of knowing, he meant something specific. In Scripture, Jesus prayed that we would come to know his Father (John 17:3). And the Greek word used in his prayer is *ginōskō*—a verb that connotes "familiarity acquired through experience."[37]

To move from knowing *of* God to *knowing* him, we must experience him personally—with our hearts.

That's the whole point of the journey.

■ ■ ■

In the early 1960s, the US Air Force renamed the Experimental Flight Test Pilot School at Edwards. It was to be called the Aerospace Research Pilot School (ARPS) to reflect the country's shifting focus toward manned spaceflight. Borman was among the first class of pilots to matriculate at ARPS. He also helped develop a new aircraft just for the new program: the NF-104A Aerospace Trainer.[38]

Jet fighter aircraft generally have altitude ceilings of forty thousand to fifty thousand feet, maybe as high as sixty-five thousand.[39] Above that, without some way of generating thrust beyond that which a jet engine can deliver, the air is just too thin for a fighter to maintain level flight. But the NF-104A did have a way. On top of its traditional GE turbojet, it was souped with a six-thousand-pound-thrust LR-121-NA-1 rocket motor. Adding rocket propulsion allowed the airplane to zip and zoom to "altitudes in excess of 120,000 feet"—positively smashing through its altitude ceiling.[40]

■ ■ ■

In the decade or so before my Oregon/Montana/Colorado journey, I was able to stockpile a pretty decent understanding of God's love—in my head. I read all those amazing words in Scripture describing it. I read and heard many wise and learned people writing and speaking about it. But I also know now that I hadn't much sensed or experienced God with my heart.

I needed to go. I needed to encounter God for myself—with the heart instrument God had given me. And when I did, he filled me with rocket fuel. The rocket fuel of his love. So when I returned home, my ability and my willingness to listen to him, to trust him, and to follow him—in all moments, even the toughest—went *way* higher.

I went way higher. I smashed through the altitude ceiling that had been limiting my life and my relationship with God. That journey four years ago equipped me to break into limitless skies above.

"Even youths shall faint and be weary, and young men shall fall exhausted; but they who wait for the LORD shall renew their strength; they shall mount up with wings like eagles" (Isa. 40:30–31).

■ ■ ■

We gain head knowledge by hearing or reading about a thing. We gain heart knowledge by going and experiencing the thing for ourselves. We gain heart knowledge of another person by going and meeting him or her. And we get to know that person quickly and deeply when we go and meet him or her and then do something together. Take a road trip. Share in an adventure. Embark on a shared quest.

Jenn and I got the opportunity to lead three mission trips to Tecate, Mexico, on behalf of our church. And we found consistently that we were able to develop deeper and more enduring friendships with other families over nine days in the mountains than in nine years of attending church together back home. Our hearts connected more easily *out there.*

We get to know other people quickly and deeply by sharing rough roads and long days. By sharing hardship and boredom. By arguing, laughing, and sharing meals and wide-ranging conversations. By putting ourselves into situations where we have to rely on and trust one another. By putting ourselves into situations where we can learn from one another.

Borman got to know Jim Lovell quickly and deeply on Gemini VII. Their mission was to test the impact on the human body of long durations in space. Their flight lasted thirteen days, eighteen hours, thirty-five minutes, and one second, according to the mission clock.[41] It was six days longer than any previous spaceflight, and it stood as a record for nearly five years.[42]

Crew quarters were tightest on Gemini flights. Among Mercury, Gemini, and Apollo spacecraft, the Gemini capsule was the smallest in terms of cubic feet per astronaut.

"Borman and Lovell were cooped up in a spacecraft smaller than the front seat of a Volkswagen Bug," wrote Kranz, and they were "virtually immobile for fourteen days."[43]

Sharing that kind of experience, Borman figured, "they would either hate each other or become friends."[44] But the cramped space wasn't all they had to share. "I don't know how in the world we could, but in that small area … we lost a toothbrush."[45]

After splashdown, a helicopter plucked the astronauts from the sea and flew them to the USS *Wasp*, a nearby aircraft carrier, for debriefings and medical exams. When they stepped onto deck, Lovell joked, "We'd like to announce our engagement."[46]

Astronauts Frank Borman and Jim Lovell Arrive aboard the Aircraft Carrier USS *Wasp* after Gemini VII

We get to know people by encounter, by experience, with our hearts. With little or no specific awareness of it, *that* is how we gather data—evidence of them, evidence of relationship, evidence of love.

Moments and memories. And none of it requires we understand other people fully. We could know them for a lifetime and never get our hands around the complexity of them, never figure out their deepest places.

But we can know them truly. And love them fully.

The same is true of God. No matter how hard we try, we'll never fully figure him out. We'll never be able to quantify or calculate or compute him. No matter how much we learn, there will always be more mystery.

But we don't need to comprehend him to know or love him. We humans can "know God truly," in our hearts, while never knowing him "comprehensively" or "exhaustively," wrote Vern Poythress from Westminster Theological Seminary.[47]

And we get to know him as we do any human person—not by scientific or intellectual exercises but with our hearts, by *doing things together*, person to person.

■ ■ ■

If we want to experience God, we need to be open and curious, ready to learn, ready to be surprised—ready for anything—because God might do anything. We must be ready for and open to new experiences and new ideas. We must be patient and observant and let God do his thing—whatever that is, whenever he wants. We must be ready for and open to the natural *and* the supernatural. The physical *and* the spiritual.

If we aren't, we'll likely miss what he does. And we might very well miss *him*. (I sure have.)

And that's why the spiritual practice of journeying is a prime method of encounter. When we hit the road or head off into the wilderness or embark on a pilgrimage, we put ourselves (and our heart instruments) into states of readiness and openness. Readiness and openness are the very essence of exploration and adventure.

Our hearts are much less likely, by contrast, to be ready and open at home. At home we build walls and biases to protect and isolate ourselves. We create schedules and systems that provide comfort and security and predictability. We develop thought habits that can close us off from new ways of thinking. We develop habits of action (and addictions) that distract us and allow us to avoid or deny pain and loss and regret, to numb the guilt and shame of our sin.

And relationships are hard to build in all that—especially with God. It's hard to sense him in the midst of our crazy busyness and our well-established coping mechanisms. Our hearts are less sensitive to the Holy Spirit when we're driving from task to task, meeting to meeting, call to call. It's futile to try to sense his presence and hear his voice when we're almost mindlessly moving from post to post, link to link, show to show.

Home has a kind of gravitational pull—pulling us away from God, pulling us down into well-worn ruts, down into comfort, but into confusion and distraction and dullness too.

But by crossing the thresholds of our homes, then of our hometowns and possibly our home countries, we leave behind what gets in the way. When we embark on a journey, when we walk unfamiliar paths in new territories, then we can break free, at least temporarily, from the infrastructure that defends us, that helps us survive and get through a day, but that stultifies and inhibits relationship too.

Going on a journey is an act of surrender. It's also an act of exchange. Jesus said, "Whoever loses his life for my sake will find it" (Matt. 10:39). When we surrender the valuable things of this world, even for a time, we get what's *most* valuable in return. When we surrender our habits, our expectations, and the overstimulation that dulls our heart instruments, then we get to sense and experience the subtle and supernatural, the marvelous and miraculous. When we surrender *home*, we get to go after "a far better country … *heaven* country" (Heb. 11:16).[48]

As pilgrims, our focus narrows to the present, our next steps. We're able to be present to each moment. Able to pay attention and awaken to wonder. In the desert, in the wilderness, on the road, all of a sudden, we have time. We have time to look for God. Time to listen for his voice. Time to meet him. And our heart instruments become sensitive. We see things we normally wouldn't. A star. A face. A need. And we hear things. A train whistle. An unexpected conversation. A whisper. And we feel things. A breeze. A handshake. A stirring in our hearts.

"A spiritual kingdom lies all about us," wrote Tozer, "enclosing us, embracing us, altogether within reach of our inner selves, waiting for us to recognize it. God Himself is here waiting our response to His Presence."[49]

But it's going to require some risk and some commitment.

Embarking on a sacred journey, taught Richard Rohr, is "a matter of leaving behind." "It's letting go of an old world so a new world can happen."[50]

Borman said, "The view of the Earth from over the lunar horizon was certainly significant for me. But by the same token I love the view of the Bighorns on a cold morning."[51] What he meant, in the context of the interview, was that God is present *everywhere*. He is in heaven—*and* he is here. He watches from his throne—*and* he lives among us, in us. "He doesn't play hide-and-seek with us. He's not remote; he's *near*. We live and move in him, can't get away from him!" (Acts 17:27–28).[52]

So while it might be easier to meet him on the road or in the wilderness, he'll meet us at home too. If we're ready and open, willing to get out of our comfort zones, we *can* be pilgrims anywhere. "Not everyone can go on physical pilgrimage," wrote Charles Foster. "But everyone can have the mind of the nomad-disciple."[53]

That said, we should, if at all possible, choose to be *physical* pilgrims. If we can, we should pick up and start walking or get into our cars and get moving or get on airplanes and get going. But if those things are too difficult—because of obligations or limitations—we should, then, choose a *hybrid* approach, embarking on metaphorical journeys punctuated by a few shorter physical journeys (spiritual retreats or weekends alone somewhere, for example). And if even hybrid journeys are not possible, then surely we should be metaphorical pilgrims.

NOTE: Sometimes the choice is not our own. Sometimes we're forced into figurative journeys, metaphorical deserts, by our circumstances—often tough, unwanted circumstances. But that kind of journey can be as sacred as any other, often more so, *if we choose to use the journeys as opportunities to meet God.*

It took guts to sit on top of a Saturn V rocket. It remains to this day the tallest (363 feet), the heaviest (6 million pounds), and the most powerful rocket ever used. It is "5 and a half million pounds of high explosive," marveled Jim Lovell.[54]

But it took a special kind of guts to refire the third stage of a Saturn V.

During the first stage, five engines blew 7.7 million pounds of thrust and lifted the spacecraft to an altitude of 40 miles and to a speed of five thousand miles per hour. The first stage then separated—to fall into the ocean. Then a different set of five rocket engines propelled the craft during the second stage, this time to an altitude of 115 miles and a speed of 15,500 miles per hour. Then the second stage separated.

The third stage had only one rocket engine. It boosted the spacecraft into low Earth orbit—to an altitude of approximately 120 miles and to a speed of roughly 17,500 miles per hour. Once there, the third stage shut down temporarily. It was refired only when the crew and the folks at mission control decided they were go for translunar injection (TLI)—the process of propelling astronauts and their craft away from Earth toward the moon.

It was TLI that made Apollo 8 so risky. When Borman, Lovell, and Anders refired Saturn V's third stage, there was no turning back. They were riding a gigantic firecracker into a great unknown—into the frightening and fascinating frontier of cislunar space.

And their course calculations had to be right. "Too low," Borman said, "would have plunged us into the moon. If our trajectory had been too high," he said, "we would have been flung into space, doomed to circle aimlessly until we ran out of oxygen."[55]

Borman: *"9, 8, 7 ... 4, 3, 2... Ignition."*
Lovell: *"Ignition."*
Mission Control: *"Roger. Ignition."*[56]

The astronauts relit the third stage and let it burn for about five minutes, taking them up to more than 23,000 miles per hour.[57] At that speed, it would still take them more than two and a half days to reach the moon.

Mission Control: *"You're on your way. You're really on your way!"*[58]

■ ■ ■

George MacDonald's mythical story "The Golden Key" is the tale of a journey. In it, two characters, Mossy and Tangle, set out to discover a deeper, unseen reality.

They set out toward God.

Of the two, Tangle struggled to sense and trust what's unseen. As a result, her path was more roundabout than Mossy's. But near the end, in a cave, she encountered a character named the Old Man of the Earth.

He pointed the way forward. He guided her into the next leg of her adventure:

> Then the Old Man of the Earth stooped over the floor of the cave, raised a huge stone from it, and left it leaning. It disclosed a great hole that went plumb-down.
>
> "That is the way," he said.
>
> "But there are no stairs."
>
> "You must throw yourself in. There is no other way."[59]

There *is* no other way. The journey is waiting. Are *you* willing to take some risks? Are you willing to make a commitment? Are you willing to let go of an old world, even temporarily, so you can reach a new one?

If so, we first need to get down to earth. We need to address some practical questions—about schedules and destinations and preparation, things like that. So that's what's coming in the next chapter, chapter 6.

— ON BOARD —

"BECKONED"

005

We modern Christian men take things at second- or thirdhand far too much. We've gotten too content with knowing of God and heaven and the spiritual realm through the eyes of other people. But we aren't designed for that.

We're designed to see and hear and touch things for ourselves. We're wired to get our hands dirty and our feet wet. Because we're more comfortable, somewhere deep in our human mechanics, trusting—and acting on—knowledge we obtain firsthand. We consider firsthand knowledge more likely to be rooted in truth; we consider it more representative of what is *real* and what is *right*.

Relationships with God that are based on firsthand knowledge, therefore, tend to be more dynamic, more durable. By contrast, faith lives built solely on secondhand knowledge tend to get stale over time. A bit wobbly.

So it's time to stop settling for the accounts and opinions of others. It's time to stop making life decisions based on the experiences and convictions of authors and pastors and friends. *And it's time to go*. It's time to go *out there* and confirm for yourself that the presence behind the sacred mysteries is who he says he is.

Consider these questions and capture your responses.

005.1 How do you know God? Do you know him directly, or do you know *of* him indirectly? Do you know him more with your head or with your heart?

Pull out a pen or pencil and circle the number below that reflects your answer:

<< More with my head - - - - - - - - - - - - - - - More with my heart >>

1 2 3 4 5 6 7 8 9 10

005.2 What might be getting in the way of encountering, experiencing, knowing God? Anything? Hurt? Disappointment? Passed-down assumptions? Stubborn biases? Have you ever told God that he just doesn't interact with his sons and daughters anymore? Or maybe it's busyness? Your schedule? Is there time in your daily calendar to encounter him? Or is it habits? Addictions? Coping mechanisms? Self-protection? Entertainment? Comforts? What in your life could be contributing to confusion, distraction, dullness?

As you ponder these questions, ask the Holy Spirit for help. Pray as King David prayed: "Search me, O God, and know my heart! Try me and know my thoughts! And see if there be any grievous way in me, and lead me in the way everlasting!" (Ps. 139:23–24).

Create a bulleted list that honestly reflects the obstacles that might exist in your heart or your life.

005.3 Can you recall a time in your past (or a few) when you were able to get out of your comfort zone, out of your zones of security and predictability? Times when you hit the road and went somewhere—either literally or figuratively—and had a significant spiritual experience? Times when you sensed something happening in your heart, something supernatural? What happened? How did it feel?

Write a few sentences about each experience.

005.4 Phil Cousineau, author of *The Art of Pilgrimage*, asked his readers, "Have you ever made a vow to go someplace that is sacred to you, your family, your group? Have you ever *imagined* yourself in a place that stirred your soul like the song of doves at dawn?"[60] I ask that of you now. Is your heart pulling you in a particular direction? Is there a place you've always wanted to go? Where you've promised yourself that you *would* go if you ever found the time? Have you ever had a "big idea"—ever longed to do something you've never done?

Write a few sentences about what comes to mind. And consider this: Could the wanderlust in your heart have been placed there by God?

Pray right now:

Jesus, you showed us how to journey. I want to journey too. I want to go. To see. To feel. To draw closer to you. To meet our Father. Please help me clear the path, clear the calendar, clear the clutter in my life. Through your Spirit in me, speak right to my heart. Help me appreciate how you ***have*** *been speaking already. Light a fire in my heart. And lead me further. Lead me on.*

Amen.

Engage in listening prayer.* God wires into each of us, into our hearts, certain desires, interests, motivations, and ambitions. He designs us to be drawn to certain places and things. And he knows that wiring infinitely better than we do.

So let's ask him about it.

---

* Again, for a full explanation and discussion of listening prayer, please refer to chapter 3 in the first book in the WiRE Series for Men, *Invention: Break Free from the Culture Hell-Bent on Holding You Back.*

Find a place where you can sit still comfortably for thirty minutes or so. The quieter, the better. Invite the Holy Spirit to direct your thoughts. Pray against distraction, against fatigue, against confusion. Now, remain quiet for a length of time—whatever feels right. Just breathe and relax. Enjoy the moments of solitude. Then, when you're ready, close your eyes and ask God this question:

> *Are you calling me somewhere? To a certain place or activity, to a specific journey or adventure, to a particular pilgrimage or quest?*

Let thoughts come. Listen *inside*. Listen for an inner voice—for God's "still small voice" (1 Kings 19:12).[61] Don't rush it. Take plenty of time. Ten to twenty minutes, at least.

When we engage God in this way, he's sure to answer at some point, in some way—probably in one we won't expect. He can be as creative and inventive as he wants to be.

But if you struggle to hear, don't sweat it. His answers might not come right away. They may come later—in a conversation or while reading a book or watching a movie or in some other moment of clarity. So if you struggle, don't dwell on it. Just keep your eyes and ears open. And keep trying. Maybe commit to engaging in listening prayer every day for a week or a month. You'll be surprised, I am sure, by what you're able to hear.

And when you do see or hear or sense something—a picture, a word, a whisper, an impulse—make sure to write it down. Again, this is precious data. And remember also, test it against Scripture. And trust the insights of friends who are mature believers.

OXYGEN AND BEAUTIFUL SILENCE AND ENCOUNTER

Time is tight. But it's *always* tight when the mission clock is running. There's just so much everyone wants to accomplish. The folks back in Houston schedule every minute and every move—and astronauts have to try to keep up. But that's not so easy when you're walking and working in this crazy, hard-to-get-used-to one-sixth gravity.

And these two moonwalkers have got a bit behind.

A little more than twenty-four hours ago, the commander and his lunar module pilot clambered out of the command module into their lunar module. They dropped out of orbit and touched down on the gunmetal-gray surface. A third man—the command module pilot—stayed back. He's now circling and piloting the craft that will, four days from now, carry all three 238,900 miles back home.

The two astronauts on the moon spent the early part of the day exploring their landing site. The mountainous southeast edge of Mare Imbrium ("Sea of Rains"). Theirs is the most scientifically oriented Apollo mission to date, and their focus is lunar geology. Some months ago, scientists at NASA surmised these peaks would be a good bet for rock samples.

The commander and lunar module pilot also just became the first astronauts to explore the moon using NASA's brand-new lunar rover—a battery-powered, eight-miles-per-hour "dune buggy."[1] This morning they dodged craters and drove out to a place called Hadley Rille—a huge meandering trench, an ancient lava channel. They also spent some time checking out the lower reaches of the Apennine Mountains.

At each spot they got out and kangaroo leaped around—which, it turns out, is the best way to move in minimal gravity. They also collected lots of rocks. Their excursion covered 5.6 miles out and back.[2]

But that was before. Now the men are back at their landing site, and the task before them is to set up some scientific equipment. Among the stuff they brought with them is the Apollo Lunar Surface Experiments Package (ALSEP). The ALSEP has multiple geophysical sensors, a radio transmitter, and a small nuclear power plant. It's designed to stay behind long after these guys leave—collecting (and beaming to Earth) approximately nine million instrument readings per day.[3]

But the darn thing won't deploy.

To save space, the ALSEP is packed in collapsed form. It's spring-loaded, and the key to setting it up is pulling two cotter pins. And that job was given to the lunar module pilot. The pins themselves, though, are underneath the machine and too small to easily grab with clumsy gloves. So the engineers at NASA attached strings to the pins.

And both strings just broke.

"So there we were," the astronaut will write years later. "The [ALSEP] was sitting on the surface of the moon, and I couldn't get two little cotter pins out."[4] But instead of getting on the radio to Houston—the constant in-ear companion of every NASA astronaut ever—the man decides to do something a bit different. He decides to pray.

Talking to God isn't this man's go-to tendency. But he does it now for a specific reason. Ever since they landed in this strange place, he's been experiencing something odd and quite surprising—"something that none of his technical training had prepared him for."[5]

What he's been experiencing is "an overwhelming sense of the presence of God."[6]

"It was a strange feeling," the man will recall later. "Almost from the time we landed, and all the way back, I was acutely aware of a holy presence."[7]

There, on the silent surface of the moon, he knows it in his heart. He knows that he knows. "God was there with us. Of that I am certain," he will later report.[8]

The presence felt so immediate, the man will also later confess, that one time he actually "turned around and looked over his shoulder"—out of sheer instinct—to see whether someone was standing there.[9]

The lunar module pilot is a Christian—but, he would say, a nominal one. He started following Jesus when he was young. But, somewhere along the line, he got more focused on career than on any kind of relationship with God. He went to school. He started flying airplanes. He became a test pilot, then an astronaut. He became a "nuts and bolts" type guy—one who, if he's honest, has gotten "rather skeptical about God."[10]

But now he's on the moon experiencing something real and surprising—and he's in a bind. He's running out of time. Those cotter pins are down there somewhere, and he can't see them. He's going to have to get ahold of them somehow—but he doesn't have time to mess around. And whatever he does, he's got to be careful. There's a layer of dust on the moon's surface, three inches thick. And it's super fine and clingy—volcanic rock ground down over eons by relentless impacts of meteoroids and interstellar atomic particles.*

If he gets down on the ground, where he might be able to get a look at those pins, he'll get covered in dust and will inevitably bring it back into the lunar module. And those maddening moon particles are brutal on noses and lungs—and they get into and ruin mechanical and electrical instruments.

So ... he prays.

Astronaut: *"God, I need your help right now."*[11]

Right then, a thought comes. He needs to "get down on one knee, holding [himself] with one hand," while he takes "the pins out with the other hand."[12]

The man trusts it. And although astronauts know they aren't supposed to manipulate sensitive equipment with their hands—because NASA scientists worry they might damage things—he gets down on one knee and works the cotter pins loose with his fingers, "bulky gloves and all."[13]

The ALSEP central station erects itself—pops "right up, three feet high."[14]

The lunar module pilot is Jim Irwin, and it's dawning on him that what he thought was an epic space voyage is actually something much larger. It's becoming, for him, a grand spiritual adventure—a journey of journeys.

---

* Oxygen is the most abundant element on the moon. But it's not in the barely there lunar atmosphere. It's locked, chemically, in lunar surface materials—in moon rocks. Nearly all the rocks found there are about 45 percent oxygen (by weight).

Jim Irwin on the Moon, Saluting the American Flag on August 1, 1971, during the Apollo 15 Lunar Surface Extravehicular Activity at the Hadley-Apennine Landing Site

■ ■ ■

At 10:56 p.m. (EDT) on July 20, 1969, Neil Armstrong stepped off the Apollo 11 lunar module ladder and sank his left boot into the powder of the southwestern shore of the Sea of Tranquility—about six hundred miles to the southeast of where Scott and Irwin would land two summers later.

With that footstep, Armstrong became the first man on the moon. And that's when he spoke his famous words: "That's one small step for man, one giant leap for mankind."[15] Historian Arthur Schlesinger Jr. called the moment the most significant event of the entire twentieth century.[16]

Twenty-seven years prior, though, a twelve-year-old Jim Irwin warned his mother that *he* might be the first man on the moon.[17] He was wrong. He would be the eighth.

Irwin was born in Pittsburgh, Pennsylvania, and that's where he became interested in flying. Dreaming, no doubt, of the pilots battling in the skies over Europe and in the Pacific, he and his family would "go out to the county airport to watch the planes take off and land."[18]

For his middle and high school years, his family moved to Salt Lake City, Utah. After graduating, Irwin went to college in Annapolis, to the US Naval Academy, where he studied naval science. Upon graduation, he joined the US Air Force.

He began flying planes in Texas—first at Hondo Air Base near San Antonio, then at Reese Air Force Base in Lubbock. Irwin then transferred to Yuma Air Force Base in Arizona. And there, on that desert tarmac, among the tumbleweeds, he saw a fleet of P-51 Mustangs—"the hottest planes I had ever seen in my life."[19] A P-51 is a prop-driven fighter-bomber with a "mighty engine" packed into "a long, pointed nose," which was so big that it "cut off your view when you were landing or taxiing on the runway."[20]

Flying a P-51 Mustang was "unbelievable."[21] And Irwin was hooked. "From that point on," he wrote, "I found myself living to fly."[22] He soon graduated from props to jets—a jet trainer, the T-33 Shooting Star, and a jet bomber, the B-45 Tornado.

At some point, like so many of his NASA brethren, Irwin decided he wanted to become a test pilot. But to qualify, he needed a graduate degree. So he headed to the University of Michigan and earned a master's in aeronautical and instrumentation engineering.

He got his acceptance to the test pilot school at Edwards in 1960—after a stint at Wright-Patterson Air Force Base in Ohio, where he worked on missile design. After his graduation, Irwin stayed on at Edwards as a test pilot and got assigned to a special, brand-new, top-secret airplane—the Lockheed YF-12. The YF-12 could reach Mach 3 and was setting new speed and altitude records.

But then, in April 1966, NASA called. The agency selected Irwin to be among the nineteen-man-strong fifth group of astronauts. His first big assignment was to back up Apollo 12—the second moon landing. Then he got to be lunar module pilot for Apollo 15.

According to the mission clock, Irwin logged 295 hours, 11 minutes on the Apollo 15 mission and 66 hours, 55 minutes on the moon.[23] He also "traveled 17.5 miles in the first car that humans have ever driven on the moon" and "collected more than 170 pounds of lunar samples."[24]

But the most remarkable thing about his moon shot for him, by far, was his encounter with God.

He called it his "baptism in the fiery power of the rocket."[25]

■ ■ ■

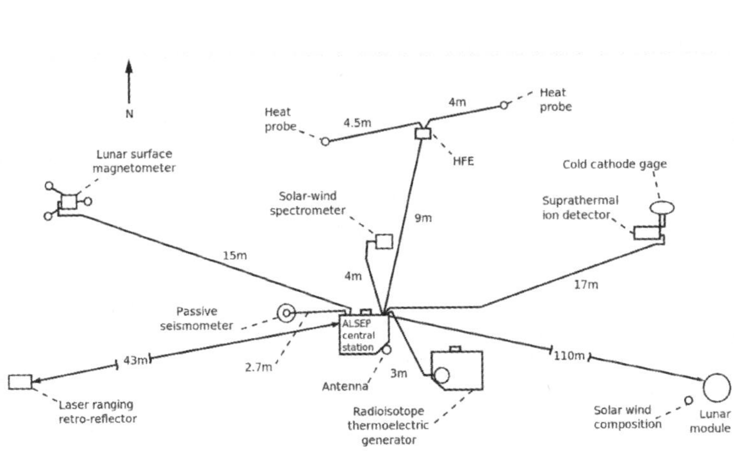

ARRANGEMENT OF THE APOLLO LUNAR SURFACE EXPERIMENTS PACKAGE (ALSEP) FOR APOLLO 15

QUESTiON:

"HOW CAN I TAKE A JOURNEY NOW?"

You may have asked … What kind of journey is even possible, given my circumstances? Where would I go? What would I do? What would happen? Isn't going on a pilgrimage something people did a long time ago? What if God doesn't show up?

You may have asked … Shouldn't I try something like this later, when I'm not so busy?

These are great questions, and the truth will blow your mind. **Think bigger.**

■ ■ ■

For all the supposed we-don't-need-God, figure-it-out-ourselves ability that our modern culture claims, shouldn't things be getting better for us? That *was* the promise.

But since the 1960s, we have become more anxious and depressed, lonelier, less connected, more medicated, more obese, and more willing to end our own lives.[26] Despite wondrous breakthroughs in science and technology, many of the trend lines that plot how we're doing as a people are getting scarier. Radical godlessness, which may have seemed so modern and broad minded, so sophisticated and progressive in prior decades—isn't working.

Here's the truth: the data looks desperate because we're wired to need God desperately. We are, each of us, designed to experience his presence in our everyday lives. We're made to let him in. Every one of us humans is built to do life with him every day.

And when we don't, we suffer.

So only one thing will change the cruel direction of those trend lines. The data is macro, but the solution is micro. The stubborn inclination of the lines on all those graphs will begin to turn when one of us, then two, then more and more, go out and actually encounter God. For it's only *with him* that we can bend those slopes. And it starts when one of us takes steps toward establishing a close, personal relationship with him.

It all starts when one of us, with and through God, escapes the surly bonds of this crazy world and begins to live the life for which he or she is meant.

It's not about what our neighbors or church members or countrymen need to do. It's not about persuading other people to be better men and women of faith. It's about each of us lighting out for the territory. Each of us, separately, hitting the road, heading off into the wilderness—to encounter for ourselves the God of heaven.

Because, as bad as things look, none of our problems is too big or too complex for God. Not one of them is too much for Elohim. El Shaddai. The Alpha and the Omega. But to access his help, we've got to get humble, be willing to adopt we-really-do-need-God, let's-figure-it-out-together attitudes.

As the apostle Paul knew, "I can do all things through him who strengthens me" (Phil. 4:13). *We* can do all things too. *Through him.*

■ ■ ■

The horizon line is calling—and we *will* find God if we move toward it.

But if we're going to make that move, we need to get practical. We need to leave the abstract, the symbolic behind. We need to ask, *What does this kind of journey actually look like in a life?* There is not going to be a single answer—and indeed, the discernment of the journey is part of the journey. But this section will help put language and detail to something that is so difficult to describe.

Will it satisfy every question for you? No, and that's the point.

But will it get you started well? Yes. And that's the point.

Where and when should we start? That's easy. We should begin *here and now*—where we are, as we are. We should each drop a pin to mark our current geographic locations, our present circumstances, our current habits and obligations. And those pins should be our points of immediate embarkation.

We must avoid the kind of thinking that says we need to get somehow fixed up before we set off toward God. We need to fight the impulse to wait until we get better—until we've dealt with our fear or sadness or anger, with our feelings of alienation, isolation, underutilization, resignation, or stagnation.

Instincts to delay can be strong. But the truth is, only grace—only the power of God to do what we can't—will ever convert those things we're dealing with into these: peace and joy and love, connection, community, purpose, resolve, and momentum. So if we wait, if we put off encounters with him, we simply delay the miraculous.

Are there different kinds of sacred journeys? Yes. The details of our journeys will look as different as we do. But there are three broad types. The first is the physical-and-spiritual journey. On these journeys, our outward and inward odysseys parallel each other. As we walk or drive or fly, as the land changes around us, so do our hearts.

For example, God might invite us to grab a pack and walk the Pacific Crest or the Appalachian Trail or the Camino de Santiago—maybe to heal from a loss. Or to take a trip to our childhood homes or to the places of our ancestral roots or to Yosemite or Denali or to work in a refugee camp in northern Baja—maybe to learn how to forgive ourselves. Or to jump on an airplane and walk the Holy Land or work for a season in a hospital in Addis Ababa or in an orphanage in Kampala or with rescued slaves in the Philippines—maybe to experience the fierce love of God. Or anything else in any number of other amazing places.

The second type is the spiritual-only journey. These are accomplished entirely through practices engaged in, at, or near our homes. For example, God might invite us into a period of authentic community with other Christian men. Or into a stretch with a Christian spiritual director or psychologist. Or into a season of simplicity. Or one of returning to a favorite childhood activity. Or of trying something of which we've always been afraid. Or into a season of creating something or leading something. Or one of consistent prayer or deep Bible study or regular meditation on Scripture. Or any number of other wonderful things.

And the third type is the hybrid journey. These are a blend of the first and second types, and they can fall anywhere between the two extremes. For example, God might invite us into some sort of interior journey and have us remain mostly at home but then enrich and enliven our journeys with a series of shorter physical trips.

For example, God might invite us to go on a short-term mission trip to an inner city, followed weeks later by a men's retreat at the beach, followed by a silent retreat in the mountains, followed by a visit to an estranged family member. Or he might invite us to take a fishing or hunting or camping or mountain biking trip alone for a few nights. Or to take a trip somewhere to do some sort of prayer or to fly to meet with a friend or mentor for a few days or to attend a particular conference or a new church. Or, again, any number of other awesome and worthwhile things.

Given the nature and pace of modern life and given important and legitimate obligations like jobs and marriages and children, hybrid journeys are common.

But whatever type of journey God invites us into, he seems to organize them around somewhat narrow themes or distinct ways in which our hearts are to be transformed. That means that most or all of the experiences within any given journey, regardless of type, will typically lead to a singular advance or specific revelation or place of significant inner healing.*

He knows what we need most. He understands our situations, our obligations, our truest desires.

He is kind.

---

* It also means there are sure to be subsequent adventures. God is sure to call us to future journeys to address other ways we need to be transformed. He'll keep calling us to himself—taking us deeper into relationship and continuing to rescue and restore our hearts and our lives. To heal us and make us whole. Again and again.

■ ■ ■

Where do we go? That's not so easy.

Most historical Christian pilgrimages have had specific destinations. Jerusalem. Mount Sinai. Rome. Nazareth. Ephesus. Santiago de Compostela. Iona. Wittenberg. La Villa de Guadalupe. Lourdes. Adventurers of old would drop everything and begin walking. They hoped they might be healed or purified or saved by getting close to a particular location or relic connected with Jesus or an esteemed saint of the church.

But the rocks and the hills, the churches and the cathedrals, the bricks and the bones—they were never the point, not really. The point of any sacred journey is and has always been to encounter God. Somehow, someway, to encounter his goodness, his love, his power—himself. The sights and artifacts just helped us get our minds around the idea of his presence in the physical world.

But God *is* present here, now. Everywhere. And we meet him most often and most easily not when he makes himself available through hallowed relics or venerated landmarks, but whenever we make ourselves available to him. Wherever we might be. We meet him most often and most easily when we slip the gravity of our intense busyness and old habits and outworn thinking, even temporarily, and listen within our hearts for the voice and direction of the Holy Spirit.

So we should go wherever he leads. Even if it's not across well-known lands and along deep-rutted roads. For the Holy Spirit is a trustworthy guide. We won't get the chance to examine routes or charts ahead of time—but he knows the twists and turns, the curves and contour lines. And he'll always point us toward true north. Like a compass needle pointing toward Earth's magnetic north pole, the Holy Spirit will point our hearts toward God. Toward encounter. Toward relationship. Toward answers to our deepest questions.

Saint Irenaeus, a Greek bishop in the second century, encouraged something called *apavia,* which is a Latin word meaning "roadlessness."[27] He taught that we should strive for "a state of complete trust in the direction of God rather than human decision."[28]

Celtic Christian pilgrims in the fifth and sixth centuries embraced this idea. They undertook a kind of pilgrimage called *peregrinatio pro Christo*—which means "traveling or sojourning abroad for Christ."[29] It means leaving home without the destination fixed, seeking divine direction along the way. Some daring old Celtic chancers went so far as to jump into small boats without rudders or oars—called coracles—entrusting themselves to "the currents of divine love."[30]

Because God is everywhere, more important than *where we go* is our posture *when we go*. The most important thing is that we be ready and open. The most important thing is that we're prepared to listen to and trust and follow God's invitations and directions—whatever they are, whenever they come.

> Trust in the LORD with all your heart,
>   and do not lean on your own understanding.
> In all your ways acknowledge him,
>   and he will make straight your paths.
>   (Prov. 3:5–6)

If we will. If we accept God's invitation and cross the thresholds of our comfortable, predictable lives and go—even for a time—wherever he calls. Into uncertainty. Into mystery. Into wonder. Then he will surely lead us into deeper encounters with himself, into a richer experience of his love, and into a world of infinite possibilities.

God's taken Jenn and me and our family on a few physical journeys. He's shown us his glorious creation—as we've trekked into the backcountry of Yosemite, Lassen, Death Valley, Zion, Grand Teton, Yellowstone, Glacier, Jasper, Kenai Fjords, and Wrangell–St. Elias National Parks. He's taken us hiking along the Lost Coast, cycling around the Ring of Kerry, and up into the Uinta Mountains on horses.

He's taken us to Rome and Jerusalem. Shown us Nazareth and Jericho. Masada and the rock-cut churches in Lalibela. He's introduced us to people in the favelas of São Paulo, to members of the Navajo Nation, to Maasai tribespeople, to street kids in northern Baja, to the Missionaries of Charity in Addis Ababa, to drug addicts in the Tenderloin of San Francisco, and to Luo orphans on the shores of Lake Victoria.

He's also coupled these physical journeys with spiritual ones—like teaching me how to discover more of my true identity, who he created me to be and become; how to heal from the deep grief from my mother's death; how to live with more transparency (and freedom) with my family and friends; how to overcome the idol of money and live a life of service and significance; and how to jump into his glorious adventures, trusting him when he calls me out of my comfort zones.

■ ■ ■

On the border between the John Muir and the Ansel Adams Wildernesses, near the crest of the Sierra Nevada mountain range, there's a lake named for American inventor Thomas Edison. A creek feeds the lake from the east and flows from it to the south. It's named for the Native American tribe whose people still inhabit the surrounding areas. And each autumn, the German brown trout that dwell in Lake Edison head up Mono Creek to spawn.

In the fall of 2009, three friends and I spent a few days and nights in the vicinity of the High Sierra. We fly-fished Mono Creek and caught and released a few of those big browns. But we also took horses from a nearby pack station and rode down western slopes—to fish the south fork of the San Joaquin, into which Mono Creek flows.

Our guide for the trip, Bucko Davis, is a member of the Mono tribe. He wore a long black canvas duster and a brown cowboy hat (with a feather tucked into the band). He also carried a hatchet.

And the way he took us, there were no trails.

Bucko knew the land. He'd been a packer in those mountains for thirty years. But he still used blazes to track our path—so we could find our way back. A *blaze* is "a mark made on a tree by cutting the bark so as to mark a route."[31] And trail blazing is the ancient practice of marking routes through otherwise unmarked wildernesses.

Backcountry explorers today often use chalk or paint on bark; reflective markers nailed or tacked to tree trunks; stakes or flags driven into the ground; ribbon or flagging tape tied to tree branches; or cairns, which are carefully arranged piles of rocks.

When done properly, blazes are made at eye level—or even higher in areas that might get snow—and they follow one another at less-than-exact distances. The important thing is that, from each blaze, one can see the next somewhere in the distance.

On our 2009 trip, from his saddle, Bucko would make small, periodic slashes on trees all the way down to the area where we fished. Before we'd lose sight of the last one, he'd make a new blaze farther along.

■ ■ ■

God often works on a need-to-know basis, giving us only our immediate next steps. He goes before us, blazing trails, calling us forward, guiding us. "The steps of a man are established by the LORD," sang King David (Ps. 37:23). Our paths are "blazed by GOD" (v. 23).[32]

A blaze or trail marker in the context of a sacred journey is a nudge or a whisper or some other kind of invitation or guidance from the Holy Spirit. And when we see one and if we go to it (and do whatever he invites us to do), he'll then make another blaze somewhere out there ahead for us to find, indicating the next place to go or the next thing to do. He makes the way plain—at least as far as the next blaze.

Our work as wanderers and pilgrims, then, is to be attentive and attuned to the Holy Spirit. Our role is to follow him from blaze to blaze. Again and again and again. Anywhere. Our job is to be willing to stray from worn trails. To be willing to walk unfamiliar roads. To be willing to go even to the most unlikely of places—and to be open to whatever we might find there.

Trusting the path, the blazes, is how we begin walking with God. And it's the most thrilling thing. Spending days traveling with the Creator of heaven and the earth. The Alpha and the Omega. Immanuel. Abba.

Irwin, who took up this method, journeyed with God in his post-moon days. He described it in 1970s parlance: "One great big high."[33]

■ ■ ■

On an ordinary Sunday in the fall of 2006, Jennifer and I dropped our kiddos at childcare at our church in Menlo Park, California. Jackson was about to turn five, Oliver had just turned three, and Abby was not yet one. We got them squared away and walked to the sanctuary. An usher welcomed us at the door and handed Jenn a bulletin. We smiled, said hellos, and found seats near the back—waiting for worship to start.

Jenn read the printed announcements. I sat there doing nothing, enjoying a few minutes of simplicity and calm.

The simplicity didn't last.

Jenn leaned over, still looking at the paper in her hands. "I think we're going to Africa."

I responded with a church-quiet "What!" She handed me the bulletin. I scanned words about a group headed for Ethiopia, leaving in about eight months. They would visit a village named Roggie, down in the Eastern Rift Valley, and a school in a town called Dessie, way up in the Ethiopian Highlands. And the Holy Spirit nudged me.

I just knew that I knew. God was offering a holy invitation.

I leaned toward Jenn and said, "I think we're going to Africa."

■ ■ ■

Irwin noticed a divine blaze when he was eleven years old—at a revival meeting with his family in New Port Richey, Florida.[34]

> At the end of the meeting, they gave us an opportunity to make a decision for Christ. They called it an invitation, which was a strange word to me at that time. Something just touched my soul, causing me to get up out of my seat and go forward with some others.[35]

He followed the path offered. He made a decision. But then, like so many of us, he got distracted and lost his way. "I didn't stay as close to the Lord as I should have," he recalled. "I drifted away, coming back occasionally and then straying again."[36]

Just before his trip to the moon, though, he noticed another blaze. A pastor asked him "about six months before the flight" to speak at Willow Meadows Baptist Church in Houston, and he agreed.[37] Then he noticed a few more, and he followed those too. He felt prompted to join the Nassau Bay Baptist Church, also in Houston—and then to share his testimony with the congregation of his new church too.[38]

And then Irwin did something very interesting. He decided to pack a poem written by John Gillespie Magee Jr. in his Apollo 15 kit.[39] The poem is entitled "High Flight."

Magee was a World War II fighter pilot. His poem is an ode to the sanctity and sublimity of a solo test flight, on which he took his Spitfire aircraft up to thirty thousand feet.[40] It begins with "Oh! I have slipped the surly bonds of Earth." And it ends here:

> Up, up the long, delirious, burning blue
> I've topped the wind-swept heights with easy grace
> Where never lark nor ever eagle flew—
> And, while with silent lifting mind I've trod
> The high untrespassed sanctity of space,
> Put out my hand, and touched the face of God.

Irwin was getting restless. He was adopting the pilgrim mindset. He was getting more and more eager to meet God. He was telling God, with his actions, that he was willing to walk the blazed path.

So God arranged an encounter on the moon.

■ ■ ■

When we go, what do we do? We should be the explorers we are. We should be expectant (that something will happen) but without expectations (that certain things *must* happen). We should pay attention to the world around us, wherever we are. We should look hard, listen intently, and feel—both with our physical senses and with our hearts. We should be open to the *whole* of reality, to the natural and the supernatural.

We should be pilgrims. On the way, every day, we should be asking, *What is God trying to show me? What's he trying to give me? What is he trying to teach me today? How is he trying to guide me? To love me?* We should be willing to look harder at whatever is right in front of us—in any given moment. We should be willing to look again, to look underneath, to look for deeper truth.

And what we've missed, we'll begin to notice. What we've called coincidence, we'll begin to see as love and care. What we've called our own discoveries, we'll begin to see as his teaching and guidance. What we've called luck, we'll begin to see as his rescue. What we've called ordinary or ugly, we'll begin to see as extraordinary.

We may encounter God by reading or studying or meditating on Scripture. As we approach the Bible with senses awake and minds wide open, we'll see more of his brilliance. We'll sense *him* there among those precious words—showing us things we never saw before, teaching us deeper truths, loving us.

Or we may encounter him in other people. With senses awake and minds wide open, we'll begin to see his brilliance in the kindness and generosity and grace of family or friends or complete strangers.

Or in the strength and wisdom and familiarity of authentic Christian community—or even in the most unexpected of places.

Or we may encounter God in the magnificence of nature. With senses awake and minds wide open, we'll begin to appreciate the brilliance of a lightning strike deep inside a forty-thousand-foot thunderhead or how the moon looks on a bluebird day in the mountains or how a striped grasshopper stands on orange legs atop a rock in the desert. We'll begin to appreciate just how much energy and care went into each atom of creation. And how it's meant for us—to move and exhilarate, surprise and delight our hearts.

Some Apollo astronauts described the moon as "desolate," an "expanse of nothing," "forlorn," "forbidding," "hostile," a "vast loneliness."[41] But Irwin saw brilliance. Hadley Rille "thrilled my soul," he said.[42] "The great Apennines were gold and brown in the early morning sunshine. It was like some beautiful little valley in the mountains of Colorado, high above the timberline."[43]

Or we may encounter God by returning to the sacraments. Or in moments of stillness and silence. With senses awake and minds wide open, we'll begin to tune in to the brilliance of his still small voice. Or we might encounter that same brilliance in worship and movement. Or in laughter and celebration and joy.

Or we may encounter him in moments that are, as Richard Rohr described, "unfathomable, unexplainable, indescribable."[44] Followers of Jesus have been experiencing these kinds of makes-no-sense, mountaintop experiences for thousands of years. For example, we may encounter God's tangible presence—maybe kind of like Irwin did on the moon. Or we may hear words from someone that bring blazing clarity and exhilaration to our hearts. Or we may be overcome by God's goodness and love and fall to our knees in awe and gratitude. Or any number of other astonishing things.

Mountaintop experiences are an "inalienable part" of sacred journeys, wrote N. T. Wright.[45] "Deep, rich, and transforming experiences of the presence of God are not reserved for special categories of people," he continued. "They are on offer for everyone."[46] They won't happen all the time, of course. Or even, perhaps, very often. But sooner or later, if we're willing to become explorers and pilgrims, God will take each of us up the mountain and reveal something of himself—and, likely, something of us too.

■ ■ ■

When we do encounter him, what should we do? When we discover God in John or Acts or Romans. Or on a mountain or in a river or on a breeze. In a whisper, a prayer, a nudge. A nap, a meal, a conversation. A dream, a sermon, an exceptional sensation. Or somewhere else. Then we should simply respond.

That's how conversation begins. That's how relationship works. *Exchange.*

When we sense his presence or hear his voice, we should answer his questions or tell him how we feel or what we think about what we've sensed. Or ask him questions. Or ask for his interpretation. Or for forgiveness. Mostly we just need to get honest and talk. And then wait—and watch and listen again.

"God always answers, one way or another" (Job 33:14).[47] And the more we engage, the more we show up for our part in the back-and-forth, the give-and-take, the divine conversation, the deeper our relationships with him will get.

And we shouldn't be afraid to try to test things. Conversation with God, wrote Dallas Willard, is something we "can and should test by experiment."[48]

We can test conversations by comparing them to Scripture. We can test the substance of what we think we might have heard or of what we think we might have seen by setting it against the principles set forth in the Bible. If it fits within a solid interpretation of Scripture, we can trust it. We can listen to what we've heard. We can be guided by what we've seen. But if it doesn't fit, we must reject and forget it.

We can also test things according to their effects. We can test the substance of our conversations with God by offering him rapid responses—quick yeses—whenever we think he might be inviting us in a particular direction, toward a particular task, into a particular situation, or toward a particular person.

And if the effect of our actions is love—for God, for ourselves, for others—then, again, we can trust those conversations. If, however, the effect is to move us away from love, away from grace, away from kindness, away from forgiveness, then we must reject and forget whatever we thought we might have heard or seen or otherwise sensed.

And over time, by experimenting and testing, we can begin to recognize what Willard called "the *unmistakable stamp* of divine quality, spirit, intent and origination."[49] We can begin to tell when it's God voice and God's presence—and when it's not.

■ ■ ■

What if God doesn't show up? God assured us, "When you get serious about finding me and want it more than anything else, I'll make sure you won't be disappointed" (Jer. 29:13).[50] Because *us* finding *him* is what he wants most. He wants us to encounter him—and to build intimate father-son relationships.

"Starting from scratch, he made the entire human race and made the earth hospitable, with plenty of time and space for living so we could seek after God, and not just grope around in the dark but actually *find* him" (Acts 17:26–27).

But he won't force his love and attention on us. He'll honor us by not interrupting our busyness, by not terminating our rebellion. He'll honor us and wait until we want intimate relationships too. But if we decide that we do and if we have the courage to step out of our normal lives, even temporarily, and set off toward him, then it will happen. God will meet us. Sooner or later, somehow his presence will break into our lives. Just as it did with Irwin. (Well, maybe not *exactly* like that.)

"Whenever … they turn to face God as Moses did, God removes the veil and there they are—face-to-face! They suddenly recognize that God is a living, personal presence, not a piece of chiseled stone" (2 Cor. 3:16–17).

It may happen in small, subtle, easy-to-miss ways. An encouragement, a realization, a conviction. A sunrise, a verse, a word. Or it may happen in ways that are big, crazy, and impossible to miss. A miracle, a vision, a breakthrough. A voice undeniable, a sensation unbelievable, a presence indescribable.

He's waiting. Not for some special class or category of people. He's waiting for all of us. For people with busy jobs, bustling families, and bills to pay. His journeys are for *us* too. He's waiting for anyone who'll decide to go, to come—literally or figuratively.

He's waiting for you.

One of the best things we can do, if we want an encounter with God, is to ask for one. And to keep asking. Because "if we ask anything according to his will he hears us. And if we know that he hears us in whatever we ask, we know that we have the requests that we have asked of him" (1 John 5:14–15).

It was not Irwin, however, who, during his moon shot, prayed for an encounter with God; it was his wife, Mary:

> I earnestly prayed … that Jim's lunar adventure would be a powerful spiritual motivation and the beginning of a new life together. I also prayed that the Lord would not give Jim a minute's rest until he had completely surrendered his life to Him. When I finished, my heart was quiet and at peace, and sleep came easily. I had the assurance that God had heard my prayer.[51]

What if the journey gets hard? At some point it will. That's the reality of the sacred path—sometimes it gets hot and dusty, difficult and tiring. Because God, having made us, knows what we need. And he knows that sometimes we need hard. So, on somewhat rare occasions, encounters with him are sure to be tough—lovingly tough.

Quests to find the God of heaven are nearly always quests to find ourselves too—our true selves. And it's in the heat and hardship, trial and testing, that God forges us into those men. Good men. Whole men. He'll use our time on the road and in the wilderness to enlighten our minds and enliven our hearts, to grow us and guide us, to restore us and refresh us. He'll use those places to teach us how to be his sons—and then, how to be husbands to our wives, fathers to our children, friends to our friends, and leaders in our communities.

It's *out there* that we deconstruct old ways of thinking, old priorities, old doubts. It's *out there* that we discover new priorities, new ways of thinking, new faith. *Out there* that we get free of sin. That we learn how to stop hurting people and hurting ourselves. It's *out there* that God ignites our hearts. *Out there* that we become more reliable conduits of his "love, joy, peace, patience, kindness, goodness, faithfulness, gentleness, self-control" (Gal. 5:22–23).

"Count it all joy, my brothers, when you meet trials of various kinds," wrote James, the brother of Jesus, "for you know that the testing of your faith produces steadfastness. And let steadfastness have its full effect, that you may be perfect and complete, lacking in nothing" (James 1:2–4).

But in his kindness, God is not likely to put us through trials all the time—maybe not even often. But sometime he will. Maybe it'll be on our first journey to encounter him. Or maybe our second. Or maybe on the ones after that. Only he knows.

So is it ever going to get hard? Yes, it probably will. But when it does, remember, you're made for hard. You're made to go and see, to struggle and overcome—not to run and hide, to avoid and deny, to numb and succumb to your addictions. You're made to face obstacles and push through. You're made to conquer, not to cower.

And remember, when we take the pilgrim's way, we're never actually alone.

Wherever we go, we have Jesus, our mentor, who shows us how to take the journey, how to push through adversity, how to reach the goal: "Follow me and I'll show you how" (Luke 9:23).[52] And we have the Holy Spirit, our guide, who energizes and encourages and comforts us, bringing clarity, confirming truth, and pointing the way forward—who will be with us "forever" (John 14:16). And we have our heavenly Dad, our Father God, who loves and loves and loves: "I will never leave you nor forsake you" (Heb. 13:5).

We have the full Trinity with us always. And they're all in.

■ ■ ■

What do I take with me? Not much. In fact, it's more important what you *don't* take. Here's Jesus' advice: "Travel light" (Luke 10:4).[53]

Our normal lives are complicated and cluttered. And in them, it's hard to connect with God. "We lose touch with him," wrote Irwin, because we're "moving too fast."[54]

The very point of hitting the road, of heading off into the wilderness—literally or figuratively—is to gain temporary reprieve from the extravagances, the distractions of home. It's to surrender, even temporarily, the things that keep us from God, in return for something much, much better.

So the more of home we try to take with us, the more we try to insulate ourselves from the unfamiliarity, the discomfort, the boredom of our journeys, the more we will inevitably insulate ourselves from the journey itself—and, likely, from encounters with God.

Extras, luxuries, things that entertain and occupy our minds—they hinder us from experiencing what's most important. Loading up phones or tablets with lots of movies, for example, if we're going on a physical-and-spiritual journey. Or allocating too little time for solitude at home, for example, if we're taking a spiritual-only journey.

"Divert my eyes from toys and trinkets," wrote the psalmist (119:37). Such things quicken and compress our moments. They narrow and numb our awareness. Instead, the biblical author pleaded, "Invigorate me on the pilgrim way" (v. 37).

Sacred journeys should be simple. Unlike our normal lives, they should be uncomplicated and uncluttered. When they are, they get us to places where it's just us and God—no intermediaries or interference or interruptions. With as little as possible that will keep us from being present to him and to what he's doing with us and within us.

■ ■ ■

Of the Apollo 15 crew, Irwin's experience was unique. More than his crewmates, he was able to be present to what happened, in space and on the moon, because of his role.

He wrote,

> It is not an accident that the lives of the Lunar Module Pilots have been more changed by the Apollo flights than the lives of the Commanders or the Command Module Pilots. The people in my slot were sort of tourists on these flights. They monitored systems that were, for the most part, not associated with control of the vehicle, so they had more time to look out the windows, to register what they saw and felt, and to absorb it.[55]

Irwin had an easier time getting "outside of ordinary reality."[56] He was able to get out from under things that would have kept him in constant motion, busy and distracted.

He was able to surrender more. And he got more in return.

Lunar Module Pilot Jim Irwin (Left), Commander Dave Scott (Middle), and Apollo 15 Support Crew Member Joe Allen (Right) during Geology Training in New Mexico in 1970

■ ■ ■

Traveling light puts us into positions of dependence. Without the benefit of too much gear or too many provisions—without our usual coping mechanisms—we make ourselves vulnerable to deprivation and fatigue and tedium. By putting ourselves into such positions, we learn to trust God more than our stuff.

Charles Foster, whose journeys have taken him to the north pole, the Sinai and Sahara deserts, the Australian outback, Ethiopia, Mozambique, and Namibia, explained that when we trust God and travel light, we're "given a new sort of comfort."[57]

By traveling light, we surrender ourselves to God's care. We put ourselves into positions where we need his help. And when we ask him for it, he gives it. Often in surprising ways—and not always with timing that makes sense. But he gives it and always in ways that are sufficient.

And when he does, we see him more clearly. We learn who he can be for us. Each hour, each struggle, each adventure, each interaction—they deepen our understanding. As we learn to recognize and accept and enjoy his care and companionship, we learn more about who he is and how he works.

We begin to rely less on what others say and learn about him for ourselves.

■ ■ ■

What will happen to *me*? I don't know. Every person is different—and each of us is treated differently by our loving Father God.

But I can tell you stories.

Irwin gave God a little, then more, then more. And God reciprocated. His post-NASA life wasn't without pain and hardship, but it was characterized also by a massive influx of peace and joy and purpose. "Of all the Moonwalkers," wrote one journalist in 1975, "Irwin seems the most content and fulfilled."[58]

"I am more than I was before," he said.[59] "When we blasted off … I had no notion whatsoever of the spiritual voyage."[60] "I went to the moon an ordinary guy and I could have come back rich.… But I went to the moon and found God. I think I am the richest man who ever walked on that moon."[61]

His life "took on a new dimension."[62] His relationship with God changed. "Jim began to grow spiritually by leaps and bounds," wrote Mary.[63] And their marriage changed too. The Irwins became closer, more loving toward each other.[64] And his vocation also changed. "I was possessed by a growing feeling that God [had] a new mission for me."[65] He just knew that he knew that God had something bigger for him than piloting experimental aircraft—bigger and better even than going to the moon.

Mary remembered the moment when her husband saw the blaze that pointed him toward his new mission: "He was riding down the streets of New York City during his first ticker-tape parade with cheering crowds on either side: *You are a servant to all the world now*, the message came."[66]

Irwin left NASA soon thereafter. "It became more and more obvious," wrote Mary, "that Jim's purpose for living was his increasing opportunity to share his Christian faith, *not* the NASA arranged public relations tours or Apollo 17."[67]

Irwin himself wrote, "The power of God was working in me."[68] He was feeling a "growing conviction," a "terrific compulsion" to follow God's leading.[69] So, for twenty years, he and Mary traveled the world as goodwill ambassadors—meeting with everyone from elementary school students to presidents and kings, telling them about his experience and his faith.[70]

And Irwin's close, conversational relationship with God, which began on the moon, continued.[71] He experienced and enjoyed God's presence and companionship many, many times thereafter.[72]

■ ■ ■

The details are way different, of course, but my story is not unlike Irwin's.

I too have experienced my share of pain and hardship, but when I started surrendering to and traveling with God—literally and figuratively—I also experienced a massive influx of peace and joy and purpose. Those things took the place of fear and striving and boredom.

My connection to God went from weak to strong. I learned that only he can answer my deepest questions: *Who am I? Who is he? Whom did he make me to be? What does he dream I will do?* And I learned that he was eager for me to ask him those questions.

And as he did with Irwin, God began answering.*

---

* The story of discovering my God-given identity is captured in *Invention*—the first book in the WiRE Series for Men.

And the more I got to know him (and myself), the more I began to love him. I couldn't help it. He set my heart ablaze with love. And I began to love myself too. When I encountered him, experienced him, I could sense the delight in his eyes when he looked at me. I started seeing myself more as he does—and I started liking myself a whole lot more.

And then there have been those adventures together. Inward journeys. Outward journeys. Journeys to amazing places to meet astonishing people and see beautiful things. And, of course, an awesome journey into a brand-new kind of work.

In one of his books, Gary Haugen, CEO of International Justice Mission, told the story of a colleague—a heroic, Harvard-trained lawyer who's seen some crazy things and followed God to some crazy places. It's a good story. But his description of what this woman gets to experience in exchange, *because of her willingness to go*, is what struck me most. I memorized this description the first time I read it, and my friends tease me about how often I bring it up:

> And she gets to experience God. Not without struggle and scrapes and doubts. But at the end of the day her cheeks are flushed, her eyes are clear, and she has stories. She has unforgettable days with her Father on great mountains.[73]

Those kinds of days are the *best*. And I've had a few myself.

How about you? Do you want some unforgettable days?

Of course, but you might be feeling some trepidation too. Or you might find yourself asking, *Is this really going to be worth it … for me?* That's okay. It's expected. And it's what the next (and final) chapter is all about.

— ON BOARD —

"READY"

006

Getting practical is sometimes taken to mean "figuring it out ourselves." We don't want to do that. "Listen for GOD's voice in everything you do, everywhere you go; he's the one who will keep you on track" (Prov. 3:6).[74] We want God to be part of even our planning and preparation. We want to look for his blazes; we want to take his direction—even before we set off.

Consider these questions and capture your responses.

006.1 "Centuries of travel lore suggest," wrote Cousineau, "that when we no longer know where to turn, our real journey has just begun. At that crossroads moment, a voice calls to our pilgrim soul."[75]

This is your crossroads moment, my friend. Do you hear God's call? Are you ready? Are you ready to walk the blazed path? To follow his lead?

Pull out a pen or pencil and circle a number below that honestly reflects your willingness:

<< STILL PRETTY RELUCTANT - - - - - - - - - - - - - - - - - - - VERY WILLING >>

1 2 3 4 5 6 7 8 9 10

Pray right now:

Holy Spirit, help me know where to go, what to do.
Help me resist the urge to delay. Show me my first steps.
Blaze the trail for me, even now, as I plan and prepare.

I trust you. I'm listening, watching—*even now. My senses are awake. My mind is wide open.*

I need you now.

Amen.

Engage in listening prayer. Let's pray with eyes open and pen (or pencil or phone with note-taking app) in hand.

Find a place where you can sit comfortably and quietly for thirty minutes or more. Again, somewhere outside would be good, but any place will do. When you're there, invite the Holy Spirit to direct your thoughts. Pray against distraction, against fatigue, against confusion. Now, just like before, remain quiet for a period of time—whatever feels right. Just breathe and relax. Enjoy the moments of solitude. Then, when you're ready, ask God this question:

Holy Spirit, my guide, given the nature and pace of my life and given important and legitimate obligations like my job and marriage and children, what type of journey (physical-and-spiritual, spiritual-only, or hybrid) would be good and right for me to undertake?

Let thoughts come. Listen for an *inner* voice—for God's still small voice. Don't rush it. Take plenty of time. Five to ten minutes for this question alone. Capture in writing whatever you sense. And remember, his answer might not come easily and right away. It may come later—through a sermon, in a thought while shaving, in a chat with your spouse. So, in the coming hours and days, make sure to keep your senses awake and mind wide open to the whole of reality.

Now, another question. And this one's the big one:

Holy Spirit, my counselor, what journey, what adventure, what quest, what pilgrimage, specifically, are you calling me toward today? Where are you calling me to go? What are you calling me to do?

To fire your imagination, you might review the examples from earlier in this chapter. Then, again, let thoughts come. Listen for God's still small voice. Spend the rest of your time here, listening for an answer to this question. Stay with it. Write down whatever you sense. And remember, it might not be a right-away kind of thing. He may reveal his plans over a period of days, weeks, even months. So keep asking. And keep listening.

Because of the potential for affecting other people, this is not a time for recklessness or impulsiveness. As always, test against Scripture everything you think you might have heard in listening prayer. But run it all by your spouse too. And by trusted friends. Talk with your pastor. Talk with your employer, if appropriate.

Be responsible. Be considerate to the people in your life. Make sure your absence or journey commitments won't have negative consequences for them. As Charles Foster wrote, "A pilgrimage is not a selfish jaunt. It does not entitle you to say that God has commanded you to wash your hands of all responsibilities. Don't leave others to mop up the mess that you have left."[76]

Also, don't take chances with your physical safety. God wouldn't want that. And don't take chances with someone else's relational or financial well-being. He wouldn't want that either.

Take to God all your prep questions. Like what to take with you. If your journey is a physical-and-spiritual or a hybrid journey, the question of what to pack is crucial. Ask him what's essential—beyond the kit, the boots, and the wool socks. A Bible? A particular book? A phone? Ask him what's necessary and what can be left behind to travel more lightly.

Regardless of journey type, ask him what (either tangible or intangible) you can lay down for the season ahead. Certain habits, coping mechanisms, comforts, extravagances, distractions? Relationships that are unhealthy and need to be paused? Unhelpful skepticism or cynicism or expectation?

Ask him about the details of your journey. For example, if your journey is a physical-and-spiritual one, ask him about where to stay (e.g., hotel, hostel, tent) and how to travel. Mode of travel is a crucial concern for many modern Christian pilgrims.

If your journey is spiritual-only, ask him what your calendar should look like, how much time per day (or per week) you should devote to spiritual activities. Ask about whether you should be using a dedicated space in your home or elsewhere.

And no matter the journey type, ask him how best to set aside time for solitude and reflection. Ask him what you should commit to in terms of time and frequency. Ask what it should look like. And pray about how you should capture your prayers, thoughts, frustrations, elations, and sensations from these times. A travel journal? A notebook? A sketch pad? An app?

Bring him into all aspects of your preparation.

It took Irwin some time to sort out how he'd changed as a person in space. A few days after his trip, a reporter asked him what happened to him out there. "Frankly," he said to the reporters, "I don't think I have changed any. I'm still the same guy."[77]

"God was taking over my life," he wrote later, "and I didn't even realize it."[78]

"During this sort of flight," Irwin explained, "you are too busy to reflect on … the secret awakenings that come from the inner flight that takes place at the same time. You have to try to register these experiences and examine them later."[79]

That's good advice for all pilgrims. Processing takes time. It was "three weeks to a month" before Irwin "started putting things together."[80]

But, in shorter order than we usually assume, we begin to forget details—even important ones. It's vital, therefore, to do what Irwin counseled—to register our experiences for later examination. We must keep a travel log. We must write down whatever's going on, outside and inside, so we don't lose the particulars, the insights from our experiences.

If we keep a log, we'll be able to hold on to what happens to us out there. We'll be able to reexperience the marvelous moments but also process what happened underneath and beyond and above those moments too, all at an appropriate time and pace.

PHOSPHORUS AND PLANET EARTH AND UNION

The chairs in the meeting room are those steel folding kind you see everywhere. They're lined up in four rows, seven chairs each. Nearly all are occupied.

There's a man in the second row with his wife. And when a friend told him about this weekend Bible study thing, he thought, *Boooorrrring.*[1] He could get his head around reading Scripture for like half an hour or something. But studying the Bible for an entire weekend?

He'd held his tongue, though. Because he knew his wife would be interested in going. And, if he's honest, he's been hard on her over the years. His professions, his missions—they've always come first. All his absences and outbursts—she's been so "understanding and patient" with him, especially lately.[2]

So when they were invited to this weekend event, he agreed. And they came out to the T Bar M ranch on Friday evening for a brief introduction. The ranch is outside the town of New Braunfels (which is itself outside San Antonio)—and it hosts tennis camps and all sorts of other events, like this one. They came back out Saturday, all day. And they're back again today—for the final day of the course.

But it's late now. The windows are dark, the room lit only by the bright and strange phosphor-emitted light from fluorescent bulbs overhead. The instructor is wrapping up—finishing on the last book of the Bible. And the man in the second row is still engaged. He's got a great capacity for focus but only if something captures his interest. While he didn't expect it to, this program has.

It's been a two-day walk through the entire Bible, meant to provide a high-level understanding of Scripture from Genesis to Revelation. And the guy up front is pretty good. But, for the man, here's what's super weird: it's as if there's been another voice in the room—a quiet one underneath that of the instructor. A kind, strong voice. And it almost seems to be coming from within the man himself.

He sensed it yesterday, when the group was going through the Old Testament. The instructor was leading the class through the books of Isaiah and Jeremiah, talking about prophecies of a Messiah—a man "who would bring in a new covenant and who would bear the punishment of many and be put to death for the sins of the people."[3]

That's when he first sensed it: "*Charlie, who do you say Jesus is?*"[4]

Then, early this morning, they were looking at John 1: "In the beginning was the Word, and the Word was with God, and the Word was God.... And the Word became flesh and dwelt among us, and we have seen his glory, glory as of the only Son from the Father, full of grace and truth" (vv. 1, 14).

And he heard it then too: *"So, Charlie ... who do you say Jesus is?"*[5]

And the voice has been coming gently, again and again.

"Who is Jesus?"[6]

As the class ends, the instructor thanks everyone and talks about other programs his organization offers. The man and his wife shake some hands, give a hug or two, say a few goodbyes. But no one lingers. The days, while fascinating and illuminating, have been long. And everyone's ready to get home.

The man, though, is totally distracted, his mind still on that voice—those questions. He doesn't say much as he and his wife exit into the April night. It's south-central Texas humid. But, thankfully, not too hot.

They get into their automobile. The man slides his key into the ignition and pauses. After several seconds the big engine breaks the silence. The man backs out of the parking space and makes his way toward the entrance of the ranch. He stops at a stop sign, glances left, pulls onto the rural highway, and accelerates southeast toward home.

Other than the sounds of the wind and the road and the motor, the car is silent. The man is deep in thought. He's an earnest guy, and he can't ignore what's been going on in his heart. His wife stays quiet too. They've been married nearly fifteen years, and she knows those furrowed brows.

They come up behind a speed-limit-driving pickup. Barely registering its existence in his conscious mind, the man grabs the turn-signal lever—*click-clack, click-clack*—and guns it around the truck.

Once clear and cruising at top speed, he senses the voice again.

"Make up your mind, Charlie. Who do you say that I am?"[7]

This voice is persistent. But the man doesn't feel pressured. The questions seem like invitations—generous invitations. And they're right on time. Because things are falling together. Things are beginning to make sense. What the man has long *professed* to believe … he's beginning to realize … he knows it's true. *It's all true.*

He turns to his wife and blurts, "Darling, there's no doubt in my mind that Jesus Christ is the Son of God."[8]

Startled at first, then overjoyed, she brings her hands together, just in front of her face, and does a couple of mini claps. And in her soft Georgia accent, she says, "That's just what God has been waiting for you to say."[9]

More silent seconds tick by.

"Charlie, do you want to give your life to him?"

More seconds.

"Yeah. I think I do."

"Then, go ahead, hon. Whenever you're ready."

More seconds.

"Jesus, I believe you're the Son of God. I believe you are who you say you are. And I guess … I want to give you my life."

There are no "angels or flashes of light."[10] No "booming voices from heaven" or "bells, horns, or whistles."[11] But something happens. A "great peace" settles in the man's heart.[12]

The man who's driving too fast on Highway 46 is former astronaut Charlie Duke—and he just knows that he knows. And his life is never going to be the same.

■ ■ ■

Duke was born in Charlotte, North Carolina, in 1935—one of two rambunctious twins. The boys were good students. And both started high school in Lancaster, South Carolina. But young Charlie transferred to Admiral Farragut Academy in St. Petersburg, Florida—in order to increase his chances of getting into the US Naval Academy, which is where he'd decided he wanted to go for college. At Farragut, he became president of his senior class and graduated valedictorian in 1953.

And he did indeed go to Annapolis. He earned a bachelor of science degree in naval sciences, graduating in 1957. One other thing he learned at the academy, though, was that he wasn't cut out for the navy. He didn't like sailing. He was miserable on ships. But fortunately for him, he and a few other Annapolis midshipmen got the chance to fly Yellow Perils—"open cockpit, biwing seaplanes, painted bright yellow."[13] And he loved that.

So when the time came to decide where to apply for his commission, Duke went for the US Air Force. And he trained first at Maxwell Air Force Base in Alabama, then Spence Air Base in Georgia, then Webb Air Force Base in Texas, then Moody Air Force Base, back in Georgia. He was a good pilot, and when he finished training, he went to Ramstein Air Base in West Germany and flew transonic F-86 Sabres and supersonic F-102 Delta Daggers.

After three years in Europe, he returned stateside and studied at MIT, earning a master's of science in aeronautics and astronautics, graduating in 1964. And while there in Massachusetts, he met Dorothy ("Dotty") Claiborne of Atlanta. She had recently graduated from college and was staying with some friends, looking for a job. The two began dating, and before too long, they got married.

Eager to get back to flying, Duke applied to the test pilot school at Edwards. When he got his acceptance, he and Dotty moved out to the Mojave. After graduation, Duke stayed on as an instructor—flying F-101 Voodoos, F-104 Starfighters, and T-33 Shooting Stars. Then, in April 1966, along with Jim Irwin and seventeen other young men, Duke was chosen to be part of the fifth group of NASA astronauts.

One of his earliest NASA assignments was to serve as CapCom for Apollo 11. *CapCom* is the NASA reduction of *capsule communicator*—people allowed to talk over the radio with the crew of a manned NASA spacecraft. As Apollo 11 CapCom, he got to communicate with Neil Armstrong and Buzz Aldrin when they landed on the moon—and an estimated six hundred million people got to hear his southern drawl.[14]

Astronauts Charlie Duke (Left), Jim Lovell (Middle), and Fred Haise (Right) at Johnson Space Center in Houston during the Apollo 11 Lunar Landing on July 20, 1969

NASA then assigned Duke the lunar module pilot slot for Apollo 16—which lifted off from Kennedy Space Center on April 16, 1972. He and John Young, the commander of the mission, landed in the Descartes highlands—roughly seven hundred miles south of where Dave Scott and Jim Irwin landed with Apollo 15.

Duke and Young remained on the lunar surface for seventy-one hours and two minutes and conducted three moonwalks—driving the rover, setting up and conducting experiments, collecting rocks, taking pictures, and shooting video. Duke said he felt "like a kid at Christmas in a candy store."[15]

Apollo 16 Lunar Module Pilot Charlie Duke and the Lunar Rover at North Ray Crater

Duke's experience on the moon was not like Jim Irwin's, though. "It was not a spiritual experience for me at all," he wrote. "It was a technical experience."[16]

Duke, like Irwin, was a professing Christian. He called himself "a loyal churchman" who "even read from the Bible as a lay reader during the service."[17] But, he wrote, "I went to church because it was the proper thing to do and I enjoyed it. I liked the people and there was a sense of well-being. But I didn't go to church to get close to God; it was a social event."[18]

And that was the state of his faith when he returned from his moon shot and began mulling over next steps. "I had reached the top of my career at age 37," he recalled. "I was at the top of the mountain, and I wondered, is this all there is? Are there no more ladders to climb?"[19]

Duke stayed with NASA for an additional three years. He served as backup lunar module pilot for Apollo 17. But, in 1975, he decided that it was time—and that his next ladder would be in business. He thought, *I'll "start climbing the ladder of success and make my million."*[20] He became a Coors beer distributor in San Antonio, and the venture was immediately successful. "The money started flowing in."[21]

But Duke's marriage was falling apart. "We looked like the all-American family," Duke remembered. "We put on a good show. But inside, we were all dying."[22]

The couple went to church on Sundays, but neither was seeking any kind of relationship with God—"our life was really empty."[23] Duke recalled his attitude at that time: "Who needed God? Only people who couldn't make it needed God. I didn't need God."[24]

But Dotty was getting desperate:

> When we got married, I had a Cinderella-type dream that he would put me first in his life, because I put him first in my life. But from the beginning he

> did not have me first. He was very work-oriented. I got very, very depressed.[25]

Looking back, Duke said, "My love for Dotty was not very strong."[26] She had long hoped that leaving NASA would change this; it didn't. Duke put the same intensity into his new company that he had into flying and being an astronaut. It got so bad that while Duke was contemplating divorce, Dotty was contemplating suicide.[27]

Then, in the fall of 1975, the Dukes attended a weekend church retreat called Faith Alive. A group of couples came and gave their testimonies—stories of how God had answered prayers and changed lives, stories about hearing God's voice, stories about personal relationships with God, stories of finding joy and peace and purpose. The couples who spoke that weekend "just glowed with the glory of God."[28] And all of it seemed, to Dotty at least, like just what they needed. That night, "alone and kneeling" by her bed, Dotty gave her life to Jesus.[29] And everything did change—for her.

Duke remembered, "I watched her change before my very eyes."[30] "She began to put Jesus first."[31] "She … began to love me and forgave me."[32] "I watched her change from sadness to joy."[33] And those changes in his wife began to influence Duke—but slowly. It would take another two and a half years for him to get to a place of surrender.

It was in April 1978 that Duke talked to Jesus in the front seat of his car.

■ ■ ■

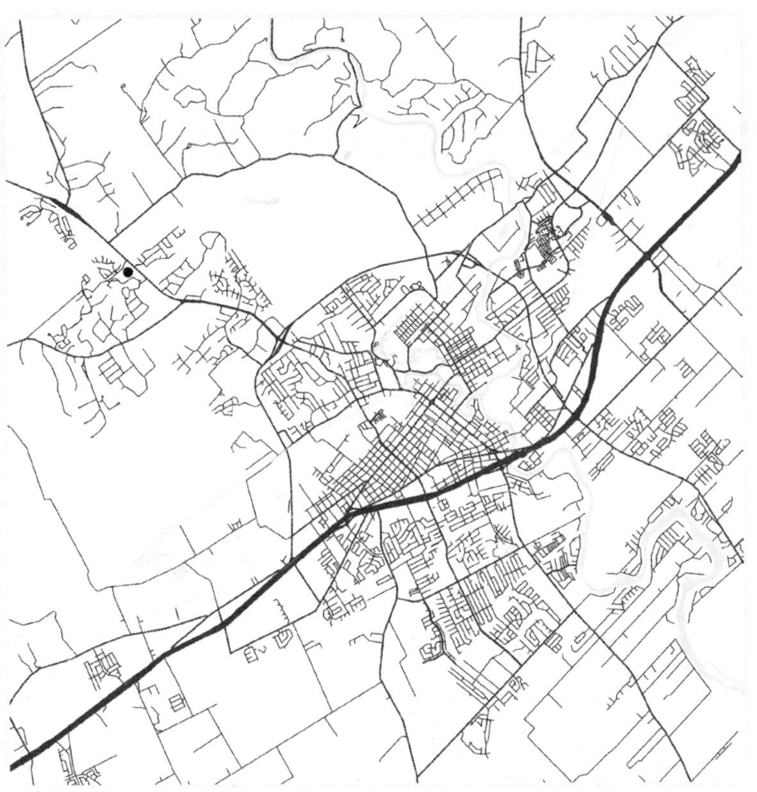

The City of New Braunfels, Texas

QUESTiON:

"IS THIS GOING TO BE WORTH IT?"

You may have asked … What difference will it make? I mean, a journey is a big undertaking. And I can calculate what it'll cost me—in time and effort. But what will I get in return—from encountering God, from building a relationship with him?

You may have asked … Is this going to be worth it?

These are great questions, and the truth will blow your mind. **Live bigger.**

■ ■ ■

The general attitude of midcentury America was a bit contradictory. Americans were confident. We'd settled into our post–World War II position as a world superpower, into the "long boom" (three decades of strong economic growth), and into a new phase of our current golden age of science, technology, and discovery.

We believed we could achieve almost any good goal to which we put our collective minds and muscles. But we were fearful too. The Cold War meant the talk in the 1950s, 1960s, and 1970s was of multiple warheads, megatonnage, Minuteman missiles, and mutual assured destruction. If the conflict ever turned hot, we knew, the outcome would be unthinkable.

Fortunately the thermometer held (for the most part). And the "war" was fought mostly with ideologies and economies. It was fought by everyday Americans stepping into their day-to-day lives with pluck and perseverance—with can-do spirits.

It was that can-do spirit that drove John F. Kennedy to throw his gauntlet down at Rice University way back in 1962. At Rice Stadium he told the world about his far-fetched plan to send an American to the moon before the end of the decade:

> We shall send to the moon, 240,000 miles away from the control station in Houston, a giant rocket more than 300 feet tall, the length of this football field, made of new metal alloys, some of which have not yet been invented, capable of standing heat and stresses several times more than have ever been experienced, fitted together with a precision better than the finest watch, carrying all the equipment needed for propulsion, guidance, control, communications, food, and survival, on an untried mission, to an unknown celestial body, and then return it safely to earth, re-entering the atmosphere at speeds of over 25,000 miles per hour, causing heat about half that of the temperature of the sun … and do all this, and do it right, and do it first before this decade is out—then we must be bold.[34]

Duke, in the air force at that time, admitted he was "incredulous" when he heard Kennedy's words.[35] *There's just no way*, he thought. *We've got 15 minutes in space with Alan Shepard's flight, and he's committing us to the moon?*[36]

But later, studying at MIT, Duke met his first group of real-life NASA astronauts. "I'd never seen anybody so enthusiastic and so positive that we were going to do this."[37]

The same can-do spirit that inspired Kennedy fueled the readiness and daring of all the Mercury, Gemini, and Apollo astronauts. Duke's fellow astronaut class member Jim Irwin wrote, "Our response was that we were always ready and able to do anything. We always said, 'We are ready, no matter what you want us to do.'"[38]

That spirit also fired the genius and grind of the NASA men and women working behind the scenes during those years—hundreds of thousands of scientists and engineers. Their culture of optimism and grit became legendary. "These teams were capable of moving right on and doing anything America asked them to do in space," said Gene Kranz.[39]

And it was that can-do spirit that enabled NASA to beat the Soviets in the space race and meet President Kennedy's goal with five months and eleven days to spare. And it's what empowered us to send five more missions to the moon, including Duke's Apollo 16.

■ ■ ■

We are, each of us, scouts and prospectors, explorers and pilgrims. We're men meant to discover and experience things for ourselves. We are men made to *go*.

And we can bring can-do to our spiritual lives.

For remember, the greatest adventures of all—the most thrilling journeys, the most fulfilling quests, the best expeditions by far—are those where God himself is the destination. The greatest adventures we'll ever undertake are the ones where we go and encounter him in the quiet sanctuary. In the darkened arena. In the ancient text. In the circle of chairs. Along the dusty trail. On the granite peak. In the grimy alley. In the orphanage or school or hospital. (Or in the front seats of our cars.)

Duke wrote,

> A number of years after my moonwalk, I began another walk—a walk with God. This experience is even more exciting than my first trip.... It has exposed me to the supernatural and mighty power of God. But most exciting of all, it has led me from a life of continual striving and restlessness to one of peace and fulfillment.[40]

Over the entire sweep of our lives, the practice of sacred journeying is among the most important things we'll ever get to do. To say it all happens on these kinds of trips is an overstatement—but not by much. The moments we spend with God on the road or out in the wilderness are outsize in their consequence. These moments shape us—as husbands, as fathers, as friends, as followers of Jesus. They influence all subsequent moments. They set up the rest of our lives—even the eternal parts.

■ ■ ■

At some point every human journey comes to an end. Every encounter too. At some point the bush stops burning, the wrestling match ends, and the road turns back on itself. We aren't meant to stay *out there* forever. Sooner or later, the time comes to leave the asphalt and the heat, the dirt and the cold, the strange smells, the new sounds, the cramped seats, the early morning flights, and the late-night trains. At some point it comes time to go home—and going home is just as important as going out.

It's as important even as encounter itself.

"Spiritual experiences, great moments of illumination and transformation, are never given simply so that we may enjoy them for their own sake," wrote N. T. Wright.[41] God allows us these journeys and the incredible moments that punctuate them for a larger purpose—for something even better, even more majestic than any single pilgrimage.

And we're able to engage in that larger purpose only once we return.

Because we come home changed.

We return home stronger, having been initiated into relationship. We come back with a new awareness—that we aren't moving through these lives, through our everyday moments, through our complex and confusing circumstances, alone. And we bring back upgraded abilities to communicate with God, having been shown how available he really is and how conversation with him actually works.

We return tougher, having been healed, not of every wound that afflicts us, but healed inwardly somehow and to some extent. For whenever we encounter God, he'll use the opportunity to father us and address one or more of the things that have been getting in the way of relationship with him—paving the way for future encounters.

And having been initiated and healed somehow and having seen God for ourselves, having glimpsed who he really is for us—how big and how good—and who we really are to him, we return with hearts ignited, with hearts afire with love and excitement.

And then, and then … we become ready to begin the *next phase.*

Charles Foster wrote, when we return home from our wanderings, "the preliminaries are over. The darkness has cleared. It is time to *begin.*"[42] And, unlike any single pilgrimage, this next phase will have no end. It will stretch seamlessly into eternity.

This next phase is a new kind of life. It's life with God. Life in the Spirit. Life in the kingdom. In it, one encounter becomes two. Two adventures become three. Knowledge becomes experience. Experience becomes relationship. Distance becomes intimacy. A vague, theoretical, intellectual concept becomes a real Father, a real friend, a real power flowing into us and through us and out into the world.

In this next phase, we become ever more able to sense his presence. Ever more able to tap into his wisdom. His guidance. His joy. His peace. His self-control. We become more equipped and eager to go ever deeper with him, ever further.

In this next phase, we become ever more able to be transformed by him. Ever more able to face and overcome the things that plague our lives. Ever more able to deal with our remaining wounds. Ever more able to deal with our remaining sin. Because of him.

"I have come to realize that Christianity is more than a ritual," wrote Duke. "It is a personal relationship with Jesus, the living God."[43] "He wants to be our friend and our counselor."[44] Relationship. Personal. Intimate. Constant.

That's the next phase. That's "newness of life" (Rom. 6:4).

It's a new kind of life. Life ignited.

But it's also … *home.* All the world becomes *home.*

■ ■ ■

Charlie Duke's pilgrimage was a hybrid journey. It was very different from Jim Irwin's physical-and-spiritual voyage—but it got him to the same place.

Duke followed the blazed trail. He didn't go climb a mountain or walk into a desert, but he took God's lead and got outside his ordinary life. He said yes ("can do") and attended that weekend event. His first steps were hesitant. But he got there. And because he did, he got to encounter God. In that unremarkable meeting room at the T Bar M ranch, he got to hear God's voice.

And then Duke's can-do attitude kicked up a few notches. His willingness to follow divine blazes picked up. First, sitting with Dotty in the front seat of their car—when he accepted God's invitation to surrender his life. Then again, the very next morning, when God led him into Scripture. He awoke with "an insatiable desire to read the Bible."[45] Before that, he wrote, "I never read the Bible."[46] "Now I couldn't put it down, and for hours a day I read the Scriptures."[47]

But that reading started out as an intellectual exercise. Duke approached it as he'd approached his coursework at Annapolis and MIT:

> As soon as I came home from work, I sat down with the Scriptures and read for hours, getting upset if I was interrupted.... My workaholic tendency was now directed toward being proficient in the Bible.[48]

By following God's blazes, though, he continued to encounter him and hear his voice—both in the words he read and in prayer. "I saw that my excessive scholarly approach to the Bible was a barrier to loving my family the way God wanted me to love them."[49]

God began fathering Duke. Counseling. Guiding. And teaching him what he wants most. More than Bible knowledge, God wants us to learn how to love—how to love him, how to love ourselves, and how to love other people.

"I realized God wanted me to read the Scriptures for the purpose of finding out what He wanted in my life," wrote Duke. "It was to be my training book and would teach me everything I needed to know."[50]

And in the midst of these encounters, God ignited Duke's heart. "I was overwhelmed by the knowledge of God and His love and power, and the desire to serve Him became a consuming fire in my heart," he wrote.[51]

And then, and then … Duke was ready to begin the next phase. He was ready to begin living a new kind of life. Life *with* God. "It was really dramatic," he said.[52] He and Dotty began experiencing "wonderful manifestations of the love and power of God, just like in the Bible."[53]

■ ■ ■

"I used to say I could live ten thousand years and never have an experience as thrilling as walking on the moon," wrote Duke. "But the excitement and satisfaction of that walk doesn't begin to compare with my walk with Jesus."[54]

And God's continued to invite him into adventures—like one to ease his grip on money and another to reassess his work priorities and another to address his drinking. And he has returned from each a changed man. God has used these to call forth the man Duke was always meant to be—and whom his family needs him to be.

God taught him how to become less self-centered, less angry. He taught him how to care about and care *for* the well-being of the people in his life. He taught him to apologize.

"God has resurrected a marriage and love that was dead," Duke wrote.[55] "We are not going full speed toward the rocks of divorce anymore," he wrote in 1990—"we're going full speed toward the peace and love of God."[56]

God restored Duke's relationships with his sons too. God taught him how to be a source of love and encouragement to his boys—rather than a source of criticism. "Our home," he wrote, "began to be a home of peace and not a home of discord."[57] "One morning while I was shaving," remembered Duke, "Tom came into our bathroom and told his mom and me, 'Things are different in our family. I like the way we are now.'"[58]

Now he and Dotty follow the blazed trail together. Wherever God's invited them, they've gone with boldness and a can-do spirit. "Since Dotty and I have given our lives to Jesus, we have seen Him direct our steps and bring situations and people into our lives that are directly God ordained."[59]

Now Duke lives a life of true adventure:

> At a Christian meeting in 1979, a prophesy was given that every step I took on the moon would be multiplied many, many times over in my walk with Jesus. This has come true in the miles I have traveled all over the world giving testimony of what God has done in my life.[60]

■ ■ ■

"Thus says the LORD: 'Stand by the roads, and look, and ask for the ancient paths, where the good way is; and walk in it'" (Jer. 6:16).

To Peter and Andrew, Jesus said, "Follow me" (Matt. 4:19). To Levi, he said, "Follow me" (Luke 5:27). To Philip, he said, "Follow me" (John 1:43). To all twelve disciples, he said, "Follow me" (Matt. 16:24).

And they did—with boldness and can-do spirits in their hearts.

To *you*, Jesus is saying, "Follow me." He's whispering it now. He wants to take you to new places—literal or figurative or both. He wants to take you to new horizons. He wants to show you things that you won't believe, that you didn't know existed—truth and beauty you didn't know were possible. He wants to bring you to himself.

He wants us to experience the "extravagant dimensions" of his love (Eph. 3:18–19).[61] The apostle Paul encouraged us to do just that: "Reach out and experience the breadth! Test its length! Plumb the depths! Rise to the heights! Live full lives, full in the fullness of God" (vv. 18–19).

God's offering you a great adventure. He's inviting you into the journey of a lifetime. He's asking whether you want to begin it today.

If you're very quiet, right now, you can hear his whisper.

Can you hear it?

■ ■ ■

Because of the power of sacred journeys, the act of stepping over the thresholds of our homes is a serious thing. Because of their potential, those first steps are different from all others.

"The threshold is more than an architectural detail," wrote Phil Cousineau. It "divides the inside from the outside, the sacred from the profane, the past from the future."[62]

The first steps on pilgrimage are weighty. And they can be difficult. (They are for me.)

First steps constitute our first moves against the inertia of home. Against our human tendencies to do nothing, to stay right where we are, to remain unchanged. Those steps are in the face of all the forces conspiring to keep us at home, in familiarity and predictability and comfort. We take them when we're still within the magnetic fields of our homes—when the magnetic pull is strongest.

So, to overcome these fundamental forces, we must be *bold.*

■ ■ ■

"Boldness has genius, power, and magic in it," wrote William Hutchison Murray, World War II–era champion of Scottish mountaineering.[63]

"Whatever you can do, or dream you can, begin it," he wrote in the travelogue of his 1950 expedition to the Himalayas.[64]

Murray was writing about the can-do spirit.

Can-do has genius, power, and magic because it gets us moving. It gets us where we need to be. It gets us into the adventure: in over our heads, beyond self-sufficiency and control.

In his classic work *The Pursuit of God*, A. W. Tozer speculated about qualities that defined and differentiated the great saints—Moses, Isaiah, Elijah, David, John, Paul, Francis, Luther—men who came to know God personally and followed him.

"They differed from the average person," Tozer surmised, "in that when they felt the inward longing they did something about it."[65]

That's what made them different. *Only that.* They began. They did something. With boldness and can-do spirits in their hearts, they got out into the broad country of God. Out where anything can happen. *Out where everything worthwhile does happen.*

Duke felt that same inward longing, and he did something about it too. He began.

> You don't need to go to the moon to find God. I didn't find God in space; I found Him in the front seat of my car on Highway 46 in New Braunfels, Texas, when I opened my heart to Jesus. And my life hasn't been the same since.[66]

■ ■ ■

It started so small. With a seemingly insignificant prayer on a Tuesday evening in rural Oregon. And with a feeble yes to an invitation to pray and listen for the voice of God on a hunting trip in the wilds of Montana. But God took my pitiful can-do offerings and turned them into something epic. He took me to places I couldn't have imagined.

And that was just the beginning. For when we relent and start walking, trekking, sharing space with God, everything is always *just the beginning*—even endings. I didn't realize it on that airplane four years ago, but every expedition with God is preparation for another. Everything he is, everything he's about, is inexhaustible love. So when we offer him our yeses and head off, we step into a forever-expanding, forever-heavenly adventure.

Life ignited.

So what difference will it make? *All of it.* All the difference. It sure has for me. Did it cost me something? Yes. For joy and connection, I've had to face the ways I hurt my family, my friends, and my acquaintances—and to be willing to try to get better. For peace and freedom, I've had to give up my idols of approval and position, security and comfort. (And I'll have to give up yet more.) For purpose and significance, I had to give up a career. But what I've gotten in return is so much better and so much bigger that those real costs seem to fade into the background, into the backward distance, as I keep moving forward, following God's blazes.

Toward him.

Toward home.

■ ■ ■

Are *you* ready for the adventure of *your* lifetime? Will you step out into the broad country of God and follow the path he's blazed just for you? Will you let him ignite your life and take you home?

Will you take your first step today?

— ON BOARD —

"BOLD"

007

George MacDonald, in *Unspoken Sermons*, wrote this:

> If we will but let our God and Father work his will with us, there can be no limit to his enlargement of our existence, to the flood of life with which he will overflow our consciousness. We have no conception of what life might be, of how vast the consciousness of which we could be made capable.[67]

The time has come to be bold, to say yes to our Father God's call. With can-do spirits in our hearts, it's time to go to him—so we can experience what MacDonald described. So that we can live lives much larger, lives ignited by his love.

Consider these questions and capture your responses.

007.1 Can you imagine the end? What might it look like for you to return home? How do you *want* it to look? What in your life do you want to change? How do you need to be transformed? What newness do you need in your life? How would you like *life ignited* to look for you?

Pull out a pen or pencil or your phone—and write a few sentences describing the return for which you hope.

Engage in listening prayer. Let's ask God for inspiration.

Again, find a place where you can sit still comfortably for twenty to thirty minutes. Invite the Holy Spirit to direct your thoughts. Pray against distraction, fatigue, and confusion. And remain quiet for a length of time. Again, breathe and relax. Enjoy the welcome moments of solitude. Then, whenever you're ready, close your eyes and pray:

> *Father, Jesus, Holy Spirit, give me something I can hold on to. A picture, a promise, a word, a song, a passage from Scripture. Maybe a scene from a book or a movie. Originate a thought in my mind—something I can hold on to. Something that will set my heart aflame as I set off into the unknown.*
>
> *Amen.*

Now, let the thoughts come. Listen again for that *inner* voice—for God's still small voice. Take plenty of time. And when and if you see or hear or otherwise sense something, write it down. And, of course, test it against Scripture.

Formulate a bold move. The quirky and easy-to-identify-with Donald Miller, in his book *A Million Miles in a Thousand Years*, described "inciting incidents"—a concept he borrowed from Hollywood storytelling pros.[68]

Inciting incidents work to counter the magnetic field of home because they get us committed and moving. Rightly formulated, they're doorways through which we can't return.[69] They become our first steps into adventure.

"Until one is committed," wrote Murray, "there is hesitancy, the chance to draw back."[70] A really good inciting incident removes that chance.

An example is to tell friends about your upcoming journey. Or, even better, to host a meal marking and blessing the beginning of your pilgrimage. It would be difficult to turn around or stand down after such a dinner.

Inciting incidents also get grace involved. They get God involved. Murray wrote this in his 1951 travelogue:

> Concerning all acts of initiative (and creation), there is one elementary truth, the ignorance of which kills countless ideas and splendid plans: that the moment one definitely commits oneself, then Providence moves too.
>
> All sorts of things occur to help one that would never otherwise have occurred. A whole stream of events issues from the decision, raising in one's favour all manner of unforeseen incidents and meetings and material assistance, which no man could have dreamt would have come his way.[71]

Spend a few minutes considering: What will your bold move be? Your inciting incident? What will be your first step?

Write it down and make it happen!

Pray right now:

> *God, I want to encounter you. I want to want to. I want to trust you. So help me, please. Lead me now to where I can be taught, fathered, befriended, and loved. Lead me wherever you'd like. Guide me to you. I want to experience you. Even if the way gets hard, I want to get to know you.*
>
> *Show me the ancient paths.*
>
> *Amen.*

Now, **go**! Once you've planned, prepared, and packed (hopefully not too much), then *go* … with all your heart, soul, mind, and strength.

And if you're so moved, email me what you're planning or doing or what you did: justin@gatherministries.com. I'd love to hear!

ACKNOWLEDGMENTS

Thank you, now and always, to Jennifer, my wife and dearest friend. One of God's greatest gifts is my life of adventure with you.

Thank you to the people who have invited me, or gone with me, into the wild places of God: Nannette Camp, Courtney Wagner, Terel Beppu, Philip Durden, John Eldredge, Julie and Robert Golter, Chris Hartenstein, Stan Mishler, Bryan Taylor, Matt Toth, and many others.

Special thanks to Kevin Kim and Wendi Lord, two amazing people who believed in me and championed this book series. Thank you also to the David C Cook team: Michael Covington, Stephanie Bennett, Nathan Landry, Jack Campbell, Kayla Fenstermaker, Paul Pastor, Nick Lee, and Megan Stengel. You guys are pros. I'm honored to have such kind, talented partners.

Thank you to my mom and dad, who taught me about God—*and about love.*

Thank you to Heather and C. J. Fitzgerald, our great friends and biggest champions. Without you, nothing we do at Gather Ministries would be possible.

And to my Father, my Papa, our God in heaven, thank you most of all. Thank you for all of it.

NOTES

BEFORE YOU START

1. NIV.

CHAPTER 001: CARBON AND BLUE SKY AND HOME

1. Housefires, "Good, Good Father," by Anthony Brown and Pat Barrett, track 7 on *Housefires II*, Housefires, 2014.

CHAPTER 002: TITANIUM AND BRIGHT STARS AND WONDER

1. Thomas Paone, "A Closer Look at the *Friendship 7* Spacecraft," Smithsonian National Air and Space Museum, February 10, 2017, https://airandspace.si.edu/stories/editorial/getting-closer-look-mercury-friendship-7-spacecraft.

2. *Results of the First United States Manned Orbital Space Flight*, Manned Spacecraft Center, NASA, February 20, 1962, 161, https://ntrs.nasa.gov/archive/nasa/casi.ntrs.nasa.gov/19930074071.pdf. Transcript edited for clarity.

3. Lyndon Johnson, quoted in Paul Dickson, *Sputnik: The Shock of the Century* (New York: Walker, 2001), 117.

4. "National Aeronautics and Space Act of 1958," Pub. L. No. 85-568, 72 Stat. 426 (1958), https://history.nasa.gov/spaceact.html.

5. "Liftoff," in *John Glenn: A Hero's Life* (New York: *Time*, December 17, 2016), 24.

6. Tom Wolfe, *The Right Stuff* (New York: Picador, 1979), 95.

7. J. Edgar Hoover, "Spiritual Priorities: Guidelines for a Civilization in Peril," *Christianity Today*, June 22, 1962, 3.

8. Charles Bolden, "NASA Remembers American Legend John Glenn," NASA, video, 10:33, December 8, 2016, www.youtube.com/watch?v=cj6EkDzO1aA.

9. "An American Hero Returns to Space: John Glenn and the STS-95 Shuttle Mission News Conference on Orbit (5 November 1998)," in Roger D. Launius, *Frontiers of Space Exploration*, 2nd ed. (Westport, CT: Greenwood, 2004), 181.

10. William Pollard, "Christianity in the Space Age," in Stephen F. Bayne Jr., ed., *Space Age Christianity* (New York: Morehouse-Barlow, 1963), 27.

11. Stephen Hawking, quoted in Nick Watt, "Stephen Hawking: 'Science Makes God Unnecessary,'" ABC News, September 7, 2010, https://abcnews.go.com/GMA/stephen-hawking-science-makes-god-unnecessary/story?id=11571150.

12. Stephen Hawking, *Brief Answers to the Big Questions* (New York: Bantam Books, 2018), 28.

13. A. W. Tozer, *The Pursuit of God* (Ventura, CA: Regal Books, 2013), 56.

14. Tozer, *The Pursuit of God*, 56.

15. John Glenn, quoted in Howard Wilkinson, "John Glenn Had the Stuff U.S. Heroes Are Made Of," *Cincinnati Enquirer*, February 20, 2002.

16. John Glenn, *John Glenn: A Memoir* (New York: Bantam Books, 2000), 349–50.

17. John Glenn, "If You're Shook Up, You Shouldn't Be There," *Life*, March 9, 1962, 29.

18. *Results of the Second United States Manned Orbital Space Flight*, Manned Spacecraft Center, NASA, May 24, 1962, 104, https://ntrs.nasa.gov/archive/nasa/casi.ntrs.nasa.gov/19620004691.pdf.

19. "Glenn's 'Spots' Puzzle to All," *Cincinnati Enquirer*, February 21, 1962.

20. Bill Kaczor, "Mercury Astronauts Recall Early Space Race," *Orlando Sentinel*, May 10, 2002.

21. C. S. Lewis, *The Abolition of Man* (New York: HarperOne, 2001), 81.

22. This and the following verses in this section are taken from THE MESSAGE.

23. THE MESSAGE.

24. NIV.

25. THE MESSAGE.

26. C. M. Ward, *"The Farther We Probe into Space, the Greater My Faith": C. M. Ward's Account of His Interview with Dr. Wernher von Braun* (Springfield, MO: Assemblies of God, 1966), 4.

27. Erik Bergaust, *Wernher von Braun* (Lanham, MD: Stackpole Books, 2017), 110.

28. THE MESSAGE.

29. THE MESSAGE.

30. Pollard, "Christianity in the Space Age," 36.

31. NIV.

32. THE MESSAGE.

33. Tozer, *The Pursuit of God*, 54.

34. John Glenn, "Glenn's Faith Linked to Orbiting Galaxies," *Evening Star* (Washington, DC), December 7, 1963.

CHAPTER 003: ALUMINUM AND BLACK SMOKE AND LOVE

1. Edward H. White Sr., quoted in 114 Cong. Rec. 1571 (1968).

2. "White," *Life*, February 3, 1967, 22, https://books.google.com/books?id=b1YEAAAAMBAJ.

3. Ralph O. Shankle, *The Twins of Space: The Story of the Gemini Project* (New York: J. B. Lippincott, 1964), 160.

4. Edward White II, "Been Weightless 1,200 Times," *Life*, September 27, 1963, 88, https://books.google.com/books?id=NFIEAAAAMBAJ.

5. "General-Father Rates White a Better Pilot Than He Was," *Evening Sun* (Baltimore), June 3, 1965.

6. *NASA Program Gemini Working Paper No. 5035: Composite Air-to-Ground and Onboard Voice Tape Transcription of the GT-4 Mission*, Manned Spacecraft Center, NASA, August 31, 1965, 44.

7. "Pastor Recalls White Felt Presence of God," *Los Angeles Times*, January 30, 1967.

8. *NASA Program Gemini Working Paper No. 5035*, 47.

9. *NASA Program Gemini Working Paper No. 5035*, 52, 54.

10. "'I'm Proud of My Boy,' White's Dad Says," *Wisconsin State Journal* (Madison, WI), June 4, 1965.

11. Stephen Hawking, *Brief Answers to the Big Questions* (New York: Bantam Books, 2018), 27.

12. THE MESSAGE.

13. Richard Rohr, *On Pilgrimage: Lourdes, Holy Land, Assisi, and Rome* (Cincinnati: Franciscan Media, 2014), audio book.

14. "When Americans Say They Believe in God, What Do They Mean?," Pew Research Center, April 25, 2018, www.pewforum.org/2018/04/25/when-americans-say-they-believe-in-god-what-do-they-mean.

15. *American Piety in the 21st Century: New Insights to the Depth and Complexity of Religion in the US* (Waco, TX: Baylor Institute for Studies of Religion, 2006), 27, 29, www.baylor.edu/content/services/document.php/33304.pdf.

16. THE MESSAGE.

17. N. T. Wright, *The Way of the Lord: Christian Pilgrimage Today* (Grand Rapids, MI: William B. Eerdmans, 2014), 65.

18. Wernher von Braun, quoted in 115 Cong. Rec. 21,062 (1969).

19. 114 Cong. Rec. 1571 (1968).

20. This and the following verses in this section are taken from THE MESSAGE.

21. A. W. Tozer, *The Pursuit of God* (Ventura, CA: Regal Books, 2013), 24.

22. Tozer, *The Pursuit of God*, 24.

23. Henri J. M. Nouwen, *The Return of the Prodigal Son: A Story of Homecoming* (New York: Image Books, 1994), 116.

24. Iron Bell Music, "Sons and Daughters," by Joel Gerdis, track 9 on *God That Saves*, Iron Bell Music, 2016.

25. Brennan Manning, *The Furious Longing of God* (Colorado Springs, CO: David C Cook, 2009), 22.

26. "1523. Gil," *Strong's Exhaustive Concordance*, Bible Hub, accessed November 23, 2019, https://biblehub.com/strongs/hebrew/1523.htm.

27. Billy Graham, *The Secret of Happiness* (1985; repr., Nashville, TN: Thomas Nelson: 2002), 8.

28. Brennan Manning, *Furious Longing*, 44.

29. Phil Collins, "Lectio Divina," Bible Gateway, accessed September 9, 2019, www.biblegateway.com/resources/scripture-engagement/lectio-divina/home.

CHAPTER 004: IRON AND BURNT RUBBER AND FORGIVENESS

1. Gordon Cooper, quoted in Gene Kranz, *Failure Is Not an Option: Mission Control from Mercury to Apollo 13 and Beyond* (New York: Simon & Schuster: 2009), 14.

2. Cooper, quoted in Kranz, *Failure Is Not an Option*, 14.

3. Kranz, *Failure Is Not an Option*, 14.

4. Cooper, quoted in Kranz, *Failure Is Not an Option*, 14.

5. Cooper, quoted in Kranz, *Failure Is Not an Option*, 14.

6. Kranz, *Failure Is Not an Option*, 14.

7. Kranz, *Failure Is Not an Option*, 14.

8. Gordon Cooper, *Leap of Faith: An Astronaut's Journey into the Unknown* (New York: HarperTorch, 2000), 79.

9. Cooper, *Leap of Faith*, 79.

10. Cooper, *Leap of Faith*, 116; Gordon Cooper, "Religious Opinions of an Astronaut," *These Times*, March 1967, 15.

11. Gordon Cooper, "Flying Is in My Blood," in M. Scott Carpenter et al., *We Seven: By the Astronauts Themselves* (New York: Simon and Schuster, 1962), 54.

12. Cooper, "Flying Is in My Blood," 54–55.

13. Quoted in Cooper, *Leap of Faith*, 78.

14. Neal Thompson, *Light This Candle: The Life and Times of Alan Shepard* (New York: Three Rivers, 2005), 336.

15. Thompson, *Light This Candle*, 338.

16. Chris Kraft, quoted in Amiko Nevills, "Remembering 'Gordo,'" NASA, October 6, 2004, www.nasa.gov/vision/space/features/remembering_gordo.html.

17. Gordon Cooper, quoted in Colin Burgess, *Faith 7: L. Gordon Cooper, Jr., and the Final Mercury Mission* (Basel, Switzerland: Springer, 2016), 54.

18. *Mercury Project Summary Including Results of the Fourth Manned Orbital Flight: May 15 and 16, 1963*, Manned Spacecraft Center, NASA, May 15, 1963, 415, https://sma.nasa.gov/SignificantIncidents/assets/summary_fourth_manned_orbital.pdf. Transcript edited for clarity.

19. Gordon Cooper, quoted in "Cooper Sees Faith in God in Space Tests," *Daily Record* (Long Branch, NJ), August 4, 1964.

20. Cooper, *Leap of Faith*, 77.

21. Gordon Cooper, quoted in *Tucson Daily Citizen*, December 7, 1963.

22. Napoleon Hill, *Think and Grow Rich* (1937; repr., Auckland, NZ: Floating Press, 2008), 459.

23. "Number of TV Households and Percentage of USA Homes with Television—1950 to 1978," Television History—the First 75 Years, accessed September 5, 2019, www.tvhistory.tv/facts-stats.htm.

24. Will Storr, *Selfie: How We Became So Self-Obsessed and What It's Doing to Us* (London: Picador, 2018), 17.

25. THE MESSAGE.

26. Gordon Cooper, quoted in Francis French and Colin Burgess, *Into That Silent Sea: Trailblazers of the Space Era, 1961–1965* (Lincoln, NE: University of Nebraska Press, 2007), 259.

27. Burgess, *Faith 7*, 23; Lily Koppel, *The Astronaut Wives Club: A True Story* (New York: Grand Central, 2014) 17; and Thompson, *Light This Candle*, 216.

28. Alvin B. Webb Jr., "Flier at Long Last Fulfills Prophecy," *Arizona Republic* (Phoenix, AZ), May 16, 1963.

29. Tom Wolfe, *The Right Stuff* (New York: Picador, 1979), 115.

30. Thompson, *Light This Candle*, 207.

31. THE MESSAGE.

32. THE MESSAGE.

33. THE MESSAGE.

34. THE MESSAGE.

35. Cooper, "Religious Opinions," 15.

36. Brent Curtis and John Eldredge, *The Sacred Romance: Drawing Closer to the Heart of God* (Nashville, TN: Thomas Nelson, 1997), 91.

37. THE MESSAGE.

38. Gordon Cooper, "God Is His Co-Pilot," *Port Huron Times Herald*, March 27, 1965.

39. THE MESSAGE.

40. THE MESSAGE.

41. KJV.

42. Brennan Manning, *The Ragamuffin Gospel* (Colorado Springs, CO: Multnomah Books, 2005), 17.

43. Dallas Willard, "The Gospel of the Kingdom and Spiritual Formation," in *The Kingdom Life: A Practical Theology of Discipleship and Spiritual Formation*, ed. Alan Andrews (Colorado Springs, CO: NavPress, 2010), 53.

44. THE MESSAGE.

45. Cooper, "Religious Opinions," 16.

46. Cooper, "God Is His Co-Pilot."

47. Thomas Merton, "This Is God's Work," in *Thomas Merton in Alaska: The Alaskan Conferences, Journals, and Letters* (New York: New Directions, 1989), 73, as quoted in Brennan Manning, *The Ragamuffin Gospel* (Colorado Springs: Multnomah, 2005).

48. Henri J. M. Nouwen, *The Return of the Prodigal Son: A Story of Homecoming* (New York: Image Books, 1994), 43.

49. Printed with permission from Many Rivers Press, www.davidwhyte.com. David Whyte, "Finisterre," in *Pilgrim* © Many Rivers Press, Langley, WA USA.

CHAPTER 005: SILICON AND OUTER SPACE AND DARING

1. *The Early Years: Mercury to Apollo-Soyuz,* NASA Information Summaries, September 1991, 8, www.nasa.gov/sites/default/files/167718main_early_years.pdf.

2. *Early Years*, 8.

3. *Early Years*, 8.

4. Frank Borman, *Countdown: An Autobiography* (New York: Silver Arrow Books, 1988), 211.

5. W. David Woods and Frank O'Brien, "Apollo 8: Day 4; Lunar Orbit 9," Apollo Flight Journal, last modified April 18, 2019, https://history.nasa.gov/afj/ap08fj/21day4_orbit9.html.

6. Gene Kranz, *Failure Is Not an Option: Mission Control from Mercury to Apollo 13 and Beyond* (New York: Simon & Schuster, 2009), 245.

7. Borman, *Countdown*, 212.

8. Frank Borman, quoted in Kendrick Oliver, *To Touch the Face of God: The Sacred, the Profane, and the American Space Program, 1957–1975* (Baltimore: Johns Hopkins University Press, 2013), 102.

9. Frank Borman, quoted in Connor Boyd, "First Man to Orbit the Moon Says It Was Only Interesting for 30 Seconds—and He Couldn't Wait to Get Home to His Family," *Daily Mail*, August 31, 2018, www.dailymail.co.uk/news/article-6119059/First-man-orbit-moon-says-interesting-30-seconds.html.

10. Ivan D. Ertel and Roland W. Newkirk, *The Apollo Spacecraft: A Chronology, vol. 4, January 21, 1966–July 13, 1974* (Washington, DC: NASA, 1978), 276, https://history.nasa.gov/SP-4009vol4.pdf.

11. Borman, *Countdown*, 214.

12. Woods and O'Brien, "Apollo 8: Day 4; Lunar Orbit 9."

13. Chris Kraft, quoted in Alice George, "How Apollo 8 'Saved 1968,'" *Smithsonian Magazine*, December 11, 2018, www.smithsonianmag.com/smithsonian-institution/how-apollo-8-saved-1968-180970991.

14. Teasel Muir-Harmony, quoted in George, "How Apollo 8."

15. Samuel C. Phillips, "The Shakedown Cruises," in *Apollo Expeditions to the Moon*, ed. Edgar M. Cortright (Washington, DC: NASA, 1975), 178.

16. Mike Kordenbrock, "50 Years Later, Apollo 8 Commander Talks the Cold War, Faith, Divisiveness and American Greatness," *Billings*

Gazette, December 24, 2018, https://billingsgazette.com/news/local/years-later-apollo-commander-talks-the-cold-war-faith-divisiveness/article_40d28210-a02c-5f04-9a4a-2292c9735a19.html.

17. John F. Kennedy (speech, Rice University, Houston, TX, September 12, 1962), https://er.jsc.nasa.gov/seh/ricetalk.htm.

18. Kennedy (speech, Rice University, Houston, TX, September 12, 1962).

19. Quoted in Phillips, "The Shakedown Cruises," in *Apollo Expeditions*, 183.

20. Kranz, *Failure*, 238.

21. James Buckner, quoted in "I Saw the Evidence That God Lives: The Story behind Borman's Message from Space," *Parade*, February 23, 1969, 12.

22. James C. Hefley, *Lift-Off! Astronauts and Space Scientists Speak Their Faith* (Grand Rapids, MI: Zondervan, 1970), 118.

23. Michael J. Buckley, quoted in Gavin Hyman, *A Short History of Atheism* (London: I. B. Tauris, 2010), 16.

24. Hugh McLeod, *The Religious Crisis of the 1960s* (New York: Oxford University Press, 2007), 1.

25. Leo Rosten, "Bertrand Russell and God: A Memoir," *Saturday Review*, February 23, 1974, 26.

26. John Glenn, "Glenn's Faith Linked to Orbiting Galaxies," *Evening Star* (Washington, DC), December 7, 1963.

27. "Apollo 8 Mission: Mission Photography," Lunar and Planetary Institute, accessed May 20, 2019, www.lpi.usra.edu/lunar/missions/apollo/apollo_8/photography.

28. "Apollo 8, Mission: Mission Photography," Lunary and Planetary Institute; "Lunar Instruments," Lunar and Planetary Institute, accessed May 20, 2019, www.lpi.usra.edu/lunar/instruments.

29. Richard W. Orloff, *Apollo by the Numbers: A Statistical Reference* (Washington, DC: NASA History Division, Office of Policy and Plans, 2000), 37, history.nasa.gov/SP-4029.pdf.

30. Borman, *Countdown*, 225.

31. A. W. Tozer, *The Pursuit of God* (Ventura, CA: Regal Books, 2013), 53.

32. THE MESSAGE.

33. John Pollock, *The Apostle: A Life of Paul* (Colorado Springs: David C Cook, 2012), 45.

34. Charles Foster, *The Sacred Journey* (Nashville, TN: Thomas Nelson, 2010), 60.

35. Frank Borman, quoted in Flora Lewis, "Exploration—the Essence of Human Spirit," *Boston Sunday Globe*, January 19, 1969.

36. N. T. Wright, *The Way of the Lord: Christian Pilgrimage Today* (Grand Rapids, MI: William B. Eerdmans, 2014), 16.

37. Frederick William Danker, ed., *A Greek-English Lexicon of the New Testament and Other Early Christian Literature*, 3rd ed. (Chicago: University of Chicago Press, 2000), 199.

38. John Terry White, "Boom and Zoom: The History of the NF-104A AST" (paper, 41st AIAA/ASME/SAE/ASEE Joint Propulsion Conference, Tucson, AZ, July 13, 2005), 2, www.916-starfighter.de/Boom%20and%20Zoom_History%20of%20NF-104A%20AST.pdf.

39. Wikipedia, s.v. "ceiling (aeronautics)," last modified November 23, 2019, 3:10, https://en.wikipedia.org/wiki/Ceiling_(aeronautics).

40. White, "Boom and Zoom," 1. See also https://en.wikipedia.org/wiki/Third-generation_jet_fighter; https://en.wikipedia.org/wiki/Fourth-generation_jet_fighter; and https://en.wikipedia.org/wiki/Fifth-generation_jet_fighter.

41. Tim Furniss and David J. Shayler, *Praxis Manned Spaceflight Log: 1961–2006* (Berlin: Springer, 2007), 95.

42. Bob Granath, "Dual Gemini Flights Achieved Crucial Spaceflight Milestones," NASA, December 4, 2015, www.nasa.gov/feature/dual-gemini-flights-achieved-crucial-spaceflight-milestones.

43. Kranz, *Failure*, 158–59.

44. Meg Jones, "50 Years Ago, Apollo 8 Astronauts Orbited the Moon and United a Troubled Earth," *Milwaukee Journal Sentinel*, December 21, 2018, www.jsonline.com/story/news/2018/12/21/50-years-ago-apollo-8-astronauts-saved-1968-genesis-reading/2301420002.

45. Frank Borman, interview by Catherine Harwood, NASA Johnson Space Center Oral History Project, NASA, April 13, 1999,

https://historycollection.jsc.nasa.gov/JSCHistoryPortal/history/oral_histories/BormanF/Bormanff_4-13-99.htm.

46. Jim Lovell, quoted in Jones, "50 Years Ago."

47. Vern S. Poythress, *Theophany: A Biblical Theology of God's Appearing* (Wheaton, IL: Crossway, 2018), 100.

48. THE MESSAGE.

49. Tozer, *The Pursuit of God*, 54.

50. Richard Rohr, *On Pilgrimage: Lourdes, Holy Land, Assisi, and Rome* (Cincinnati: Franciscan Media, 2014), audio book.

51. Borman, quoted in Kordenbrock, "50 Years Later."

52. THE MESSAGE.

53. Charles Foster, *The Sacred Journey* (Nashville, TN: Thomas Nelson, 2010), xvii.

54. *First to the Moon: The Journey of Apollo 8*, directed by Paul Hildebrandt (El Segundo, CA: Gravitas Ventures, 2018).

55. Borman, *Countdown*, 210.

56. Woods and O'Brien, "Apollo 8: Day 1; Earth Orbit and Translunar Injection," Apollo Flight Journal, last updated May 19, 2019, history.nasa.gov/afj/ap08fj/02earth_orbit_tli.html.

57. Borman, *Countdown*, 203.

58. Chris Kraft, quoted in Borman, *Countdown*, 203.

59. George MacDonald, "The Golden Key," in *The Princess and the Goblin and Other Fairy Tales*, ed. Shelley King and John B. Pierce (Peterborough, ON: Broadview, 2014), 266.

60. Phil Cousineau, *The Art of Pilgrimage: The Seeker's Guide to Making Travel Sacred* (San Francisco: Conari, 2012), 13.

61. KJV.

CHAPTER 006: OXYGEN AND BEAUTIFUL SILENCE AND ENCOUNTER

1. James B. Irwin, *To Rule the Night: The Discovery Voyage of Astronaut Jim Irwin* (Nashville, TN: Holman Bible, 1982), 65.

2. *Apollo 15 Mission Report*, Manned Spacecraft Center, NASA, December 1971, 2, www.hq.nasa.gov/alsj/a15/ap15mr.pdf.

3. Charles Conrad Jr. and Alan B. Shepard Jr., "Ocean of Storms and Fra Mauro," in *Apollo Expeditions to the Moon*, ed. Edgar M. Cortright (Washington, DC: NASA, 1975), 238.

4. James B. Irwin, *More Than Earthlings: An Astronaut's Thoughts for Christ-Centered Living* (Nashville, TN: Broadman, 1983), 55.

5. Anita Fussell, "Moon Flight Changed Irwin's Spiritual Life," *Lincoln Journal Star*, January 25, 1980.

6. Fussell, "Moon Flight."

7. Jim Irwin, quoted in Andrew Fyall, "The Moon in His Pocket, God at His Side," *Pittsburgh Press*, November 3, 1974.

8. Irwin, quoted in Fyall, "Moon in His Pocket."

9. Mary Irwin, quoted in Mark Ellis, "Encounter with Jesus on the Moon Left Astronaut Changed," God Reports, March 7, 2011, godreports.com/2011/03/encounter-with-jesus-on-the-moon-left-astronaut-changed.

10. Jim Irwin, quoted in Lorna Dueck, "Lunar Experience Changes Irwin's Life," *Star-Phoenix* (Saskatoon, SK), April 27, 1985.

11. Jim Irwin, quoted in Ellis, "Encounter with Jesus."

12. Irwin, *To Rule the Night*, 71.

13. Irwin, *More Than Earthlings*, 55.

14. Irwin, *To Rule the Night*, 71.

15. Neil Armstrong, quoted in John Noble Wilford, "Astronauts Land on Plain; Collect Rocks, Plant Flag: A Powdery Surface Is Closely Explored," *New York Times*, July 21, 1969.

16. Arthur Schlesinger Jr., in Charles Fishman, "What You Didn't Know about the Apollo 11 Mission," *Smithsonian Magazine*, June 2019, www.smithsonianmag.com/science-nature/what-you-didnt-know-about-apollo-11-mission-fifty-years-ago-180972165.

17. "86124 US Air Force Pilot Interview," video, 4:12, January 17, 2018, www.youtube.com/watch?v=DvSjxlrSAIA&t=2m56s.

18. Irwin, *To Rule the Night*, 127.

19. Irwin, *To Rule the Night*, 155.

20. Irwin, *To Rule the Night*, 155.

21. Irwin, *To Rule the Night*, 156.

22. Irwin, *To Rule the Night*, 156.

23. W. David Woods and Frank O'Brien, "Apollo 15: Splashdown Day," Apollo Flight Journal, last modified March 18, 2019, https://history.nasa.gov/afj/ap15fj/25day13_splashdown.html; Brian Dunbar, "Apollo 15," NASA, July 8, 2009, www.nasa.gov/mission_pages/apollo/missions/apollo15.html.

24. Dunbar, "Apollo 15."

25. Jim Irwin, quoted in Carrie LaBriola, "Moon Trip Called God's Plan," *Journal Herald* (Dayton, OH), November 10, 1973.

26. Jean M. Twenge, "The Age of Anxiety? The Birth Cohort Change in Anxiety and Neuroticism, 1952–1993," *Journal of Personality and Social Psychology* 79, no. 6 (December 2000): 1007–21; Gerald L. Klerman and Myrna M. Weissman, "Increasing Rates of Depression," *JAMA* 261, no. 15 (April 1989): 2229–35; Andrea H. Weinberger et al., "Trends in Depression Prevalence in the USA from 2005 to 2015: Widening Disparities in Vulnerable Groups," *Psychological Medicine* 48, no. 8 (June 2018): 1308–15; Miller McPherson, Lynn Smith-Lovin, and Matthew E. Brashears, "Social Isolation in America: Changes in Core Discussion Networks over Two Decades," *American Sociological Review* 71, no. 3 (June 2006): 353–75; John Murphy, "New Epidemic Affects Nearly Half of American Adults," MDLinx, January 11, 2019, www.mdlinx.com/internal-medicine/article/3272; Laura A. Pratt, Debra J. Brody, and Qiuping Gu, "Antidepressant Use in Persons Aged 12 and Over: United States, 2005–2008," NCHS Data Brief, Centers for Disease Control and Prevention, October 2011, www.cdc.gov/nchs/data/databriefs/db76.pdf; Cheryl D. Fryar, Margaret D. Carroll, and Cynthia L. Ogden, "Prevalence of

Overweight, Obesity, and Severe Obesity among Adults Aged 20 and Over: United States, 1960–1962 through 2015–2016," Heath E-Stats, National Center for Health Statistics, September 2018, 4, www.cdc.gov/nchs/data/hestat/obesity_adult_15_16/obesity_adult_15_16.pdf; "Suicide Rates Rising across the U.S.," Centers for Disease Control and Prevention, June 7, 2018, www.cdc.gov/media/releases/2018/p0607-suicide-prevention.html.

27. Andy Freeman and Pete Greig, *Punk Monk: New Monasticism and the Ancient Art of Breathing* (Ventura, CA: Regal Books, 2007), 113.

28. Ray Simpson, quoted in Freeman and Greig, *Punk Monk*, 113.

29. Latdict, s.v. "peregrinatio, peregrinationis," accessed August 21, 2019, latin-dictionary.net/definition/29871/peregrinatio-peregrinationis; Latdict, s.v., "pro," accessed August 21, 2019, latin-dictionary.net/definition/31663/pro.

30. Christine Valters Paintner, *The Soul of a Pilgrim: Eight Practices for the Journey Within* (Notre Dame, IN: Sorin Books, 2015), 65.

31. *Oxford Dictionary of English*, 3rd ed. (2010), s.v. "blaze," 177.

32. THE MESSAGE.

33. Irwin, *To Rule the Night*, 237.

34. Irwin, *To Rule the Night*, 22.

35. Irwin, *To Rule the Night*, 134.

36. Irwin, *To Rule the Night*, 22.

37. Irwin, *To Rule the Night*, 121.

38. Irwin, *To Rule the Night*, 121.

39. "About Us," High Flight Foundation, accessed August 24, 2019, www.highflightfoundation.org/about-high-flight.

40. Abby Finkel, "'High Flight': Poetry at 30,000 Feet," Royal Air Force Lakenheath, December 11, 2016, www.lakenheath.af.mil/News/Features/Display/Article/1025699/high-flight-poetry-at-30000-feet.

41. Frank Borman, *Countdown: An Autobiography* (New York: Silver Arrow Books, 1988), 211; W. David Woods and Frank O'Brien, "Apollo 8: Day 4; Lunar Orbit 9," Apollo Flight Journal, last modified April 18, 2019, https://history.nasa.gov/afj/ap08fj/21day4_orbit9.html.

42. Jim Irwin, quoted in Tom Twitty, "Astronaut Irwin Makes First Orlando Pulpit Appearance," *Orlando Sentinel*, July 6, 1972.

43. Irwin, *To Rule the Night*, 60.

44. Richard Rohr, *On Pilgrimage: Lourdes, Holy Land, Assisi, and Rome* (Cincinnati: Franciscan Media, 2014), audio book.

45. N. T. Wright, *The Way of the Lord: Christian Pilgrimage Today* (Grand Rapids, MI: William B. Eerdmans, 2014), 66.

46. Wright, *Way of the Lord*, 67.

47. THE MESSAGE.

48. Dallas Willard, *Hearing God: Developing a Conversational Relationship with God*, rev. ed. (Downers Grove, IL: IVP Books, 2012), 134.

49. Willard, *Hearing God*, 250.

50. This and the following verses in this section are taken from THE MESSAGE.

51. Mary Irwin, *The Moon Is Not Enough: An Astronaut's Wife Find Peace with God and Herself* (Grand Rapids, MI: Zondervan, 1978), 123.

52. THE MESSAGE.

53. This and the following verses in this section are taken from THE MESSAGE.

54. Irwin, *More Than Earthlings*, 82.

55. Irwin, *To Rule the Night*, 20.

56. Irwin, *To Rule the Night*, 17.

57. Charles Foster, *The Sacred Journey* (Nashville, TN: Thomas Nelson, 2010), 137.

58. Daniel Greene, "The Moon Men Now," *Age* (Melbourne, Australia), November 8, 1975.

59. Jim Irwin, quoted in Sandra VanAmburg, "Astronaut Will Share Testimony, Tell of Moon Walk," *Gazette* (Cedar Rapids, IA), November 7, 1981.

60. Irwin, *More Than Earthlings*, 16.

61. Irwin, quoted in Fyall, "Moon in His Pocket."

62. Irwin, quoted in Fyall, "Moon in His Pocket."

63. Irwin, *Moon Is Not Enough*, 124.

64. Jim Irwin, foreword to *Moon Is Not Enough*, by Mary Irwin, 8.

65. Irwin, *To Rule the Night*, 23.

66. Irwin, *Moon Is Not Enough*, 128.

67. Irwin, *Moon Is Not Enough*, 125.

68. Irwin, *To Rule the Night*, 23.

69. Irwin, *To Rule the Night*, 22.

70. "About Us," High Flight Foundation.

71. Irwin, *To Rule the Night*, 239.

72. Fussell, "Moon Flight."

73. Gary A. Haugen, *Just Courage: God's Great Expedition for the Restless Christian* (Downers Grove, IL: IVP Books, 2008), 21.

74. THE MESSAGE.

75. Phil Cousineau, *The Art of Pilgrimage: The Seeker's Guide to Making Travel Sacred* (San Francisco: Conari, 2012), 9.

76. Foster, *The Sacred Journey*, 139.

77. Irwin, *To Rule the Night*, 21.

78. Irwin, *To Rule the Night*, 124.

79. Irwin, *To Rule the Night*, 18.

80. Jim Irwin, quoted in "Astronaut Felt 'God's Presence' on Moon," *Beckley Post-Herald* (Beckley, WV), June 17, 1972.

CHAPTER 007: PHOSPHORUS AND PLANET EARTH AND UNION

1. "A Meaningful Walk: Astronaut Charlie Duke (Apollo 16)," video, 1:15:18, June 12, 2018, www.youtube.com/watch?v=4m9G1s8X_lE.

2. Charlie Duke and Dotty Duke, *Moonwalker* (Nashville, TN: Oliver-Nelson Books, 1990), 258.

3. Duke and Duke, *Moonwalker*, 258.

4. Duke and Duke, *Moonwalker*, 259.

5. Duke and Duke, *Moonwalker*, 259.

6. Duke and Duke, *Moonwalker*, 259.

7. Duke and Duke, *Moonwalker*, 259.

8. Duke and Duke, *Moonwalker*, 260.

9. Duke and Duke, *Moonwalker*, 260.

10. Charlie Duke, quoted in Tom Fennell, "Astronaut Duke Discovers Life's Meaning in Jesus," *Star-Phoenix* (Saskatoon, SK), April 17, 1982.

11. "A Meaningful Walk"; Danielle Linneweber, "Walk on Moon No Match for Walk with God," *Daily Ledger* (Noblesville, IN), March 25, 2000.

12. Duke, quoted in Fennell, "Astronaut Duke."

13. Duke and Duke, *Moonwalker*, 32.

14. "First Moon Landing Fast Facts," CNN, last modified August 8, 2019, www.cnn.com/2013/09/15/us/moon-landing-fast-facts/index.html.

15. Charlie Duke, quoted in Michael McManus, "Astronaut Seeks Goals after Adulation and Money," *Daily Journal* (Franklin, IN), April 17, 1982.

16. Duke and Duke, *Moonwalker*, 258.

17. Duke and Duke, *Moonwalker*, 258.

18. Duke and Duke, *Moonwalker*, 258.

19. Charlie Duke, quoted in McManus, "Astronaut Seeks Goals."

20. Duke and Duke, *Moonwalker*, 238.

21. Charlie Duke, quoted in McManus, "Astronaut Seeks Goals."

22. "A Meaningful Walk."

23. Charlie Duke, quoted in McManus, "Astronaut Seeks Goals."

24. Duke and Duke, *Moonwalker*, 258.

25. Dotty Duke, quoted in McManus, "Astronaut Seeks Goals."

26. Charlie Duke, quoted in McManus, "Astronaut Seeks Goals."

27. McManus, "Astronaut Seeks Goals."

28. "A Meaningful Walk."

29. Duke and Duke, *Moonwalker*, 249.

30. "A Meaningful Walk."

31. "A Meaningful Walk."

32. "A Meaningful Walk."

33. Charlie Duke, "Astronaut Charlie Duke on the Beauty of God's Creation," July 27, 2016, in *GPS: God. People. Stories*, produced by Billy Graham Evangelistic Association, podcast, 13:05, https://billygraham.org/audio/astronaut-charlie-duke-on-moon-walk-and-faith-walk-2.

34. John F. Kennedy (speech, Rice University, Houston, TX, September 12, 1962), https://er.jsc.nasa.gov/seh/ricetalk.htm.

35. Charlie Duke, quoted in Nina Burleigh, "Moon Landing at 50: Apollo Astronauts Reflect on JFK's Challenge and the Future of Space Travel," *Newsweek*, July 2, 2019, www.newsweek.com/2019/07/19/moon-landing-50-apollo-astronauts-reflect-jfks-challenge-future-space-travel-1446902.html.

36. Duke, quoted in Burleigh, "Moon Landing."

37. Duke, quoted in Burleigh, "Moon Landing."

38. James B. Irwin, *More Than Earthlings: An Astronaut's Thoughts for Christ-Centered Living* (Nashville, TN: Broadman, 1983), 14.

39. Gene Kranz, "Space Lifeguard: An Interview with Gene Kranz," interview by Andrew Chaikin, Space.com, April 11, 2000, http://web.archive.org/web/20000818064509/http://www.space.com/peopleinterviews/apollo13_kranz_iview_000411.html.

40. Duke and Duke, *Moonwalker*, x.

41. N. T. Wright, *The Way of the Lord: Christian Pilgrimage Today* (Grand Rapids, MI: William B. Eerdmans, 2014), 67.

42. Charles Foster, *The Sacred Journey* (Nashville, TN: Thomas Nelson, 2010), 188.

43. Duke and Duke, *Moonwalker*, 265.

44. Duke and Duke, *Moonwalker*, 264.

45. Duke and Duke, *Moonwalker*, 260.

46. Duke and Duke, *Moonwalker*, 260.

47. Duke and Duke, *Moonwalker*, 260.

48. Duke and Duke, *Moonwalker*, 262.

49. Duke and Duke, *Moonwalker*, 262.

50. Duke and Duke, *Moonwalker*, 263.

51. Duke and Duke, *Moonwalker*, 268.

52. Duke, "Astronaut Charlie Duke."

53. Duke and Duke, *Moonwalker*, 271.

54. Duke and Duke, *Moonwalker*, 280.

55. Duke and Duke, *Moonwalker*, 261.

56. Duke and Duke, *Moonwalker*, 261.

57. Duke and Duke, *Moonwalker*, 263.

58. Duke and Duke, *Moonwalker*, 263.

59. Duke and Duke, *Moonwalker*, 275.

60. Duke and Duke, *Moonwalker*, 275.

61. These and the following verses in this paragraph are taken from THE MESSAGE.

62. Phil Cousineau, *The Art of Pilgrimage: The Seeker's Guide to Making Travel Sacred* (San Francisco: Conari, 2012), 83.

63. W. H. Murray, *The Scottish Himalayan Expedition* (London: J. M. Dent & Sons, 1951), 6. Murray was quoting a loose translation of Johann Wolfgang von Goethe, *Goethe's* Faust, *Part 1*, in *Marlowe's* Tragical History of Doctor Faustus *and Goethe's* Faust, *Part 1*, trans. John Anster (London: Oxford University Press, 1907), 63.

64. Murray, *The Scottish Himalayan Expedition*, 6.

65. A. W. Tozer, *The Pursuit of God* (Ventura, CA: Regal Books, 2013), 66.

66. Duke and Duke, *Moonwalker*, 281.

67. George MacDonald, “Life,” in *Unspoken Sermons: Second Series* (London: Longman, Green, 1885), www.ccel.org/ccel/macdonald/unspoken2.ix.html.

68. Donald Miller, *A Million Miles in a Thousand Years: What I Learned While Editing My Life* (Nashville, TN: Thomas Nelson, 2009), 103–4.

69. Miller, *A Million Miles*, 103–4.

70. Murray, *The Scottish Himalayan Expedition*, 6.

71. Murray, *The Scottish Himalayan Expedition*, 6.

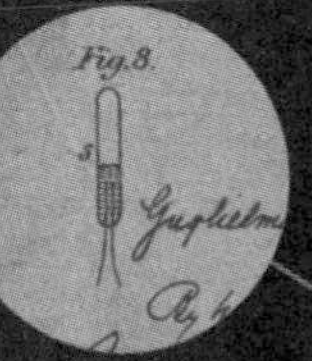

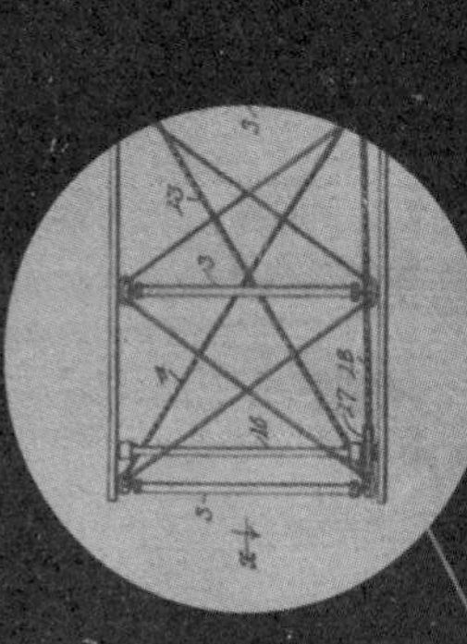

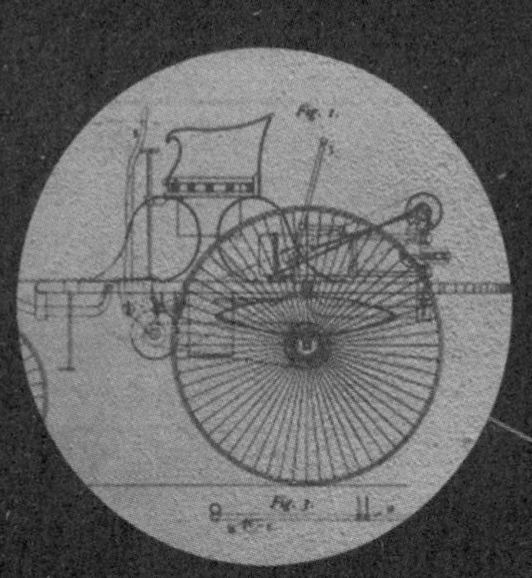